# Cool Fun Cupcakes

Fun & Easy Baking Recipes for Kids!

Alex Kuskowski

**Checkerboard Library**

An Imprint of Abdo Publishing
www.abdopublishing.com

visit us at www.abdopublishing.com

Published by Abdo Publishing, a division of ABDO,
PO Box 398166, Minneapolis, Minnesota 55439. Copyright © 2015
by Abdo Consulting Group, Inc. International copyrights reserved
in all countries. No part of this book may be reproduced in any
form without written permission from the publisher. Checkerboard
Library™ is a trademark and logo of Abdo Publishing.

Printed in the United States of America, North Mankato, Minnesota
062014
092014

Editor: Karen Latchana Kenney
Content Developer: Nancy Tuminelly
Cover and Interior Design and Production:
Colleen Dolphin, Mighty Media, Inc.
Food Production: Frankie Tuminelly
Photo Credits: Colleen Dolphin, Shutterstock

The following manufacturers/names appearing in this
book are trademarks: Gold Medal®, Kraft® Jet-Puffed®, Market
Pantry®, PAM®, Roundy's®

Library of Congress Cataloging-in-Publication Data
Kuskowski, Alex, author.
  Cool fun cupcakes: fun & easy baking recipes for kids! /
Alex Kuskowski.
    pages cm. -- (Cool cupcakes & muffins)
  Audience: 8-12.
  Includes index.
  ISBN 978-1-62403-301-8
  1. Cupcakes--Juvenile literature.  I. Title.
  TX771.K872 2015
  641.8'653--dc23
                        2013043080

# To Adult Helpers

Assist a budding chef by helping your child learn to cook. Children develop new skills, gain confidence, and make delicious food when they cook. Some recipes may be more difficult than others. Offer help and guidance to your child when needed. Encourage creativity with recipes. Creative cooking encourages children to think like real chefs.

Before getting started, have ground rules for using the kitchen, cooking tools, and ingredients. There should always be adult supervision when a sharp tool, oven, or stove is used. Be aware of the key symbol described on page 9. It alerts you when the use of a stove or oven is required and should be monitored.

Put on your apron. Taste their creations. Cheer on your new chef!

# Contents

# For the ♡ Love of Cupcakes!

Discover the wide world of cupcakes. Cupcakes come in every size, shape, and color. Cupcakes are fun to make and eat!

It's easy to make fun cupcakes that will impress others. Your friends will be amazed at your cupcake creations. Try each of the recipes in this book. Or get creative and make up your own!

This book has everything you need to get started. It's filled with fun recipes. Follow each recipe's easy steps to create tasty treats. Get inspired to create cupcakes that taste and look great!

# The Basics

## Ask Permission

Before you cook, ask **permission** to use the kitchen, cooking tools, and ingredients. If you'd like to do something yourself, say so! Just remember to be safe. If you would like help, ask for it! Always ask when you are using a stove or oven.

## Be Prepared

→ Be organized. Knowing where everything is makes cooking safer and more fun!

→ Read the directions all the way through before starting the recipe. Remember to follow the directions in order.

→ The most important ingredient is preparation! Make sure you have everything you'll need.

## Be Neat and Clean

→ Start with clean hands, clean tools, and a clean work surface.

→ Tie back long hair to keep it out of the food.

→ Wear comfortable clothing and roll up your sleeves.

→ Put on an apron if you have one. It'll keep your clothes clean.

## Be Smart, Be Safe

- Never cook if you are home alone.
- Always have an adult nearby for hot jobs, such as ones that use the oven or the stove.
- Have an adult around when using a sharp tool, such as a knife or a **grater**. Always be careful when using these tools!
- Remember to turn pot handles toward the back of the stove. That way you avoid accidentally knocking the pots over.

## Measuring

Many ingredients are measured by the cup, tablespoon, or teaspoon. Measuring tools may come in many sizes, but the amount they measure should be printed or **etched** on the sides of the tools. When measuring 1 cup, use the measuring cup marked 1 cup and fill it to the top.

Some ingredients are measured by weight in ounces or pounds. The weight is printed on the package label.

## No Germs Allowed!

Raw eggs and raw meat have bacteria in them. These bacteria are killed when the food is cooked. But bacteria can survive on things the food touched and that can make you sick! After you handle raw eggs or meat, wash your hands, tools, and work surfaces with soap and water. Keep everything clean!

# Cool Cooking Terms

Here are some basic cooking terms and actions that go with them. Whenever you need a reminder, just turn back to these pages.

## Wash

Always wash fruits and vegetables well. Rinse them under cold water. Pat them dry with a **towel**. Then they won't slip when you cut them.

## Mix

Mix means to stir ingredients together, usually with a large spoon or electric mixer.

## Whisk

Whisk means to beat quickly by hand with a whisk or a fork.

# Symbol

 **Hot!**
This recipe
requires the use
of a stove or oven.
You will need adult
**supervision** and
assistance.

# Frosting Tips

## Learn the basics of frosting fun!

With frosting the possibilities are endless. You can make frosting any color and shape you want. Check out these tips to become a master chef!

## Frosting the cupcake

1. Fill a plastic bag with frosting. Press out the extra air. Seal the bag closed.

2. Pinch one corner of the bag flat. Cut off the corner. You can cut it straight across, or in a V shape or M shape. This is the bag's tip.

3. Hold the bag with the tip pointed down.

4. Squeeze the bag to push out the frosting. Start on the outside edge of the cupcake. Go around the edge.

5. When you reach the beginning of the circle keep going. Make smaller and smaller circles. This creates a **spiral**.

6. Stop squeezing when finished.

V shape

M shape

straight
across

# Kitchen Supplies

measuring cups

mini muffin tin

measuring spoons

scoop

mixing bowls

microwave-safe bowl

spatula

electric mixer

muffin tin

glass mugs

paper liners

plastic lollipop sticks

whisk

plastic bags

mixing spoon

# Ingredients

Here are some of the ingredients you will need:

graham crackers

yellow cake mix

white cake mix

wafer ice cream cones

unsweetened cocoa powder

all-purpose flour

food coloring

whipped cream

mini chocolate
chips

chocolate
chips

non-stick
cooking spray

rock candy

chocolate
squares

mini
marshmallows

vanilla
pudding mix

vegetable
oil

honey

sour cream

vanilla
extract

marshmallow
fluff

# Bright Rainbow Cupcakes

MAKES 24 SERVINGS

## Ingredients

1 18.5-oz. white cake mix
2 eggs
1 cup sour cream
½ cup whole milk

⅓ cup vegetable oil
food coloring (red, yellow,
 green & blue)
whipped cream

## Tools

paper liners
2 muffin tins
large mixing bowl
measuring cups & spoons

whisk
5 cereal bowls
5 spoons

1   **Preheat** the oven to 350 degrees. Put paper liners in the muffin tins.

2   In a large mixing bowl, whisk together the cake mix, eggs, sour cream, milk, and oil.

3   Divide the batter evenly between the five **cereal** bowls.

4   Add 17 drops of red food coloring to one bowl. Add 13 drops of yellow and 4 drops of red to the second bowl. Add 12 drops of yellow to the third bowl. Add 12 drops of green to the fourth bowl. Add 12 drops of blue to the fifth bowl. Stir each bowl with a different spoon.

5   Put 2 teaspoons of blue batter in each muffin cup. Gently spread the batter evenly. Repeat with the other colors, going in reverse rainbow order.

6   Bake and cool the cupcakes as directed on the cake mix box. Frost the cupcakes with whipped cream.

# Hot Chocolate Delight

MAKES 4 SERVINGS

## Ingredients

8 oz. unsalted butter, softened
1 oz. unsweetened chocolate chips
6 oz. milk chocolate chips
¾ cup all-purpose flour
¾ cup white sugar
½ teaspoon vanilla extract
1 teaspoon unsweetened cocoa powder
1 teaspoon salt
4 eggs
whipped cream
mini marshmallows

## Tools

microwave-safe bowl
mixing spoon
medium bowl
measuring cups & spoons
whisk
ladle
4 large microwave-safe mugs

1. Put the butter, unsweetened chocolate chips, and milk chocolate chips in a microwave-safe bowl. Microwave on high 1 minute. Stir.

2. In a medium mixing bowl, whisk together the flour, sugar, vanilla extract, cocoa powder, salt, and eggs.

3. Add the chocolate mixture to the flour mixture. Whisk together.

4. Use a ladle to divide batter evenly between the mugs. Microwave them one at a time on high for 2 minutes. Let them cool 1 minute.

5. Top each mug with whipped cream and mini marshmallows.

# Ready to Rock 'n' Roll Cakes

## Ingredients

**CUPCAKES**
1½ cups all-purpose flour
½ teaspoon baking powder
¼ teaspoon salt
½ cup unsalted butter, softened
2 tablespoon honey
⅛ cup brown sugar
1 cup white sugar
2 eggs

2 teaspoons vanilla extract
⅔ cup cold milk

**FROSTING**
2 cups unsalted butter, softened
5 cups powdered sugar
2 teaspoons vanilla extract
2 cups crushed rock candy

## Tools

paper liners
muffin tin
mixing bowls
measuring cups & spoons

whisk
mixing spoon
plastic bag

1    **Preheat** the oven to 350 degrees. Put paper liners in the muffin tin.

2    In a large mixing bowl, whisk together the flour, baking powder, and salt.

3    Put the butter, honey, brown sugar, and white sugar in a medium bowl. Stir and then stir in the eggs, vanilla extract, and milk. Add the sugar mixture to the flour mixture. Stir well.

4    Divide the batter evenly between the muffin cups. Bake 22 minutes or until the cupcakes are golden brown. Let the cupcakes cool.

5    Make the frosting. In a medium bowl, whisk the butter and sugar until creamy. Mix in the vanilla extract. Remove the cupcakes from the muffin tins. Frost the cupcakes as shown on pages 10 and 11. Sprinkle rock candy on top of the cupcakes.

# Yummy Ice Cream Cones

**MAKES 24 SERVINGS**

## Ingredients

**CUPCAKES**
non-stick cooking spray
1 16-oz. yellow cake mix
1 box vanilla pudding mix
½ cup water
½ cup vegetable oil
4 eggs
1 cup sour cream
24 wafer ice cream cones

**FROSTING**
2 cups unsalted butter, softened
5 cups powdered sugar
2 teaspoons vanilla extract
food coloring

## Tools

2 muffin tins
mixing bowls
measuring cups & spoons
whisk

medium bowl
electric mixer
spatula
plastic bag

1   **Preheat** the oven to 350 degrees. Grease the muffin tins with non-stick cooking spray.

2   In a large mixing bowl, whisk together all of the cupcake ingredients except the ice cream cones.

3   Fill each muffin cup two-thirds full of batter. Bake 20 to 25 minutes. Let the cupcakes cool. Place a cupcake in each ice cream cone.

4   Make the frosting. Put the butter and sugar in a medium bowl. Beat with an electric mixer until creamy. Mix in the vanilla extract and a few drops of food coloring.

5   Frost the cupcakes as shown on pages 10 and 11.

# Sweet Cupcake Poppers

## Ingredients

non-stick cooking spray
¾ cup unsweetened cocoa
   powder
¾ cup all-purpose flour
½ teaspoon baking soda
¼ teaspoon salt
¾ cup unsalted butter, softened

1 cup white sugar
3 eggs
1 teaspoon vanilla extract
½ cup sour cream
2 cups white chocolate chips
½ cup multicolored sprinkles

## Tools

mini muffin tin
mixing bowls
measuring cups & spoons
whisk

mixing spoon
microwave safe bowl
small bowl
plastic lollipop sticks

1 **Preheat** the oven to 350 degrees. Grease the muffin tin with non-stick cooking spray.

2 In a large mixing bowl, whisk together the cocoa powder, flour, baking soda, and salt. Put the butter, sugar, eggs, vanilla extract, and sour cream in a medium bowl. Stir. Add the butter mixture to the cocoa powder mixture. Stir well.

3 Fill the muffin cups three-fourths full of batter. Bake 10 to 12 minutes. Let the cupcakes cool.

4 Put the white chocolate chips in a microwave-safe bowl. Microwave for 1 minute. Stir. Repeat until the chocolate is melted. Put the sprinkles in a small bowl. Dip the top of each cupcake in the melted chocolate and then in the sprinkles. Chill the cupcakes in the refrigerator 5 minutes.

5 Dip the end of a lollipop stick end in the melted chocolate. Push it into the bottom of a cupcake. Repeat until there is a stick in each cupcake. Chill the cupcakes in the refrigerator 5 minutes.

# Juicy Watermelon Cupcakes

MAKES 12 SERVINGS

## Ingredients

### CUPCAKES
1¼ cups all-purpose flour
1 teaspoon baking powder
¼ teaspoon baking soda
¼ teaspoon salt
½ cup unsalted butter, softened
½ cup white sugar
¼ cup vegetable oil
¼ cup whole milk
2 eggs
¾ teaspoon vanilla extract
½ cup mini chocolate chips
pink food coloring

### FROSTING
2 cups unsalted butter, softened
5 cups powdered sugar
2 teaspoons vanilla extract
3 drops bright green food coloring
¼ cup mini chocolate chips

## Tools

paper liners
muffin tin
mixing bowls
measuring cups & spoons

whisk
spatula
plastic bag

1   **Preheat** the oven to 350 degrees. Put paper liners in the muffin tin.

2   In a large mixing bowl, whisk together the flour, baking powder, baking soda, and salt. Stir the butter and sugar together in a medium bowl. Stir in the oil, milk, eggs, and vanilla extract. Add the butter mixture to the flour mixture. Stir well.

3   Stir in the mini chocolate chips and a few drops of pink food coloring.

4   Fill the muffin cups two-thirds full of batter. Bake 15 to 20 minutes. Let the cupcakes cool.

5   Make the frosting. Stir all of the frosting ingredients except the mini chocolate chips together in a medium bowl. Frost the cupcakes as shown on pages 10 and 11. Top with mini chocolate chips.

# S'more Surprise Bites

## Ingredients

1 cup all-purpose flour
1 teaspoon baking soda
1 teaspoon baking powder
2 cups crumbled graham
   crackers
½ cup unsalted butter, softened
1 cup white sugar

3 eggs
1 cup whole milk
½ cup mini chocolate chips
1 cup marshmallow fluff
chocolate squares
½ cup mini marshmallows

## Tools

paper liners
mini muffin tin
mixing bowls
mixing spoon
whisk

measuring cups & spoons
scoop
small bowl
spatula

1. **Preheat** the oven to 350 degrees. Put paper liners in the muffin tin.

2. Put the flour, baking soda, baking powder, and 1½ cups graham cracker crumbs in a large mixing bowl. Mix with a spoon.

3. In a medium bowl, whisk together the butter and sugar. Stir in the eggs and milk. Add the butter mixture to the flour mixture. Stir well. Stir in the mini chocolate chips.

4. Fill the muffin cups three-fourths full of batter. Bake 10 to 15 minutes or until the cupcakes are golden brown. Let the cupcakes cool.

5. Spread marshmallow fluff on the cupcakes. Put the remaining graham cracker crumbs in a small bowl. Dip the top of each cupcake in the crumbs. Put a square of chocolate and a mini marshmallow on top of each cupcake.

# Conclusion

Fun cupcakes are cool to look at and even better to eat. Making cupcakes that look amazing doesn't have to be hard. It can be easy and fun!

This book has tons of fun recipes to get you started. There's more to discover too. Check your local library for more cupcake cookbooks. Or use your imagination and whip up your very own creations!

You can make cupcakes for birthdays, holidays, or just for fun. Your friends and family will love tasting your sweet creations. Become a muffin tin chef today!

# Web Sites

To learn more about cool cooking, visit ABDO online at www.abdopublishing.com. Web sites about cool cooking are featured on our Book Links page. These links are monitored and updated to provide the most current information available.

# Glossary

**cereal** – a breakfast food usually made from grain and eaten with milk.

**etch** – to carve into something.

**grater** – a tool with rough-edged holes used to shred something into small pieces.

**permission** – when a person in charge says it's okay to do something.

**preheat** – to heat an oven to a certain temperature before putting in the food.

**spiral** – a pattern that winds in a circle.

**supervision** – the act of watching over or directing others.

**towel** – a cloth or paper used for cleaning or drying.

# Index

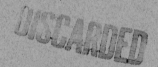

"The earth is....living poetry like
the leaves of a tree,
which precede flowers and fruit,
—not a fossil earth,
but a living earth."

—HENRY DAVID THOREAU, *WALDEN*

# VISIONS
## OF A WILD AMERICA
### Pioneers of Preservation

by Kim Heacox

Prepared by the Book Division
Published by the National Geographic Society, Washington, D.C.

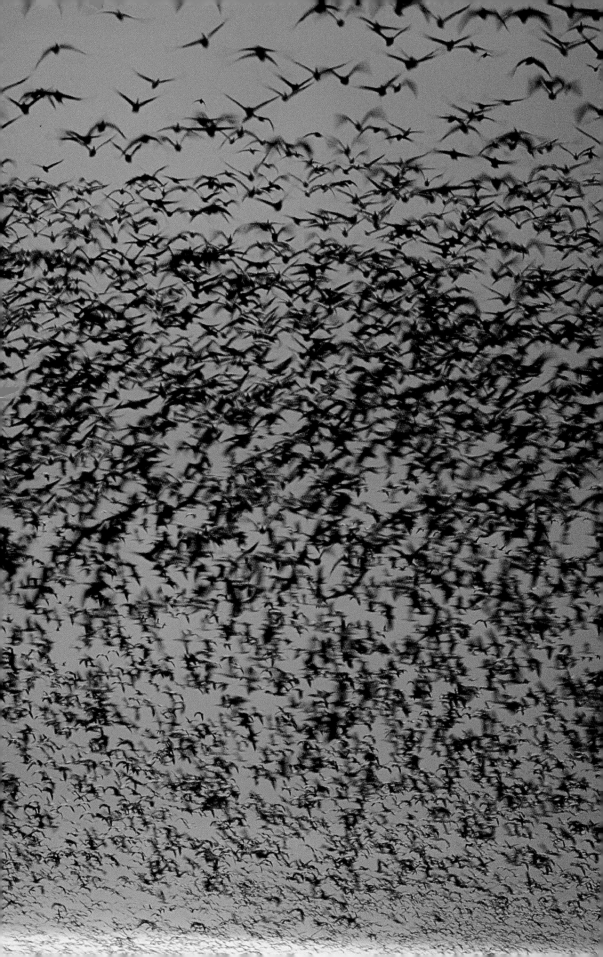

# VISIONS OF A WILD AMERICA
## Pioneers of Preservation

*By Kim Heacox*

*Published by*
The National Geographic Society
Reg Murphy, *President
    and Chief Executive Officer*
Gilbert M. Grosvenor,
    *Chairman of the Board*
Nina D. Hoffman, *Senior Vice President*

*Prepared by*
The Book Division
William R. Gray,
    *Vice President and Director*
Charles Kogod, *Assistant Director*
Barbara A. Payne, *Editorial Director*

*Staff for this book*
Martha C. Christian, *Managing Editor*
Thomas B. Powell III, *Illustrations Editor*
Jody Bolt Littlehales, *Art Director*
Victoria Garrett Jones, *Researcher*
Jane H. Buxton, *Contributing Editor*

Lewis R. Bassford, *Production Project
    Manager;* Richard S. Wain, *Production*

Meredith C. Wilcox, *Illustrations Assistant*
Kevin G. Craig, Dale-Marie Herring,
    Sandra F. Lotterman, Peggy J. Purdy,
    *Staff Assistants*

*Manufacturing and Quality Control*
George V. White, *Director*
John T. Dunn, *Associate Director*
Vincent P. Ryan, *Manager*

Elisabeth MacRae-Bobynskyj, *Indexer*

Library of Congress ℭℙ Data: page 200

*PAGE 1: Leaf shadows on the
trunk of a beech.*
*PAGES 2-3: Hiker above the clouds
in Alaska's Arctic National Wildlife
Refuge.*
*PAGES 4-5: Snow geese and
Canada geese above Nebraska,
migrating northward.*
*PAGES 6-7: Dew bejeweling a
dragonfly.*
*PAGES 8-9: Delicate Arch beneath
cloud-rippled sky in Utah's Arches
National Park.*
*PAGES 10-11: Bison amid winter
hot springs in Yellowstone National
Park, Wyoming.*
*PAGES 12-13: Yellow brittlebush,
red owl's clover, and chain cholla in
Arizona's Organ Pipe Cactus
National Monument.*

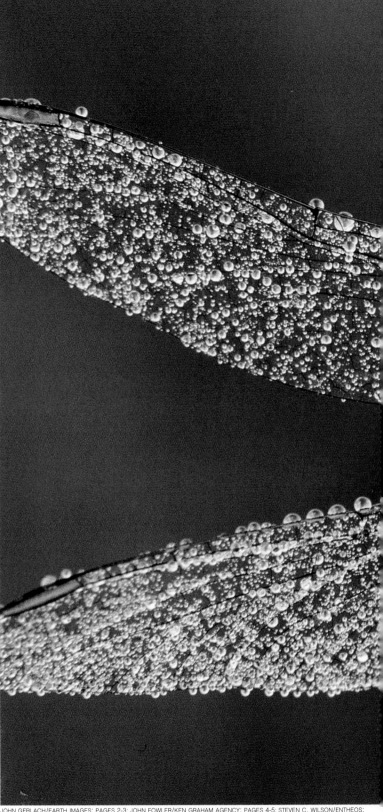

JACK DYKINGA

12

# Contents

# A DIFFERENT DRUMMER

# The Prophets of Preservation

JOHN MUIR

On March 28, 1868, a blue-eyed newcomer to California walked up San Francisco's bustling Market Street and asked a carpenter directions for the quickest way out of the city.

"But where do you want to go?" the carpenter asked.

"Anywhere that is wild," the newcomer replied.

Cities didn't suit him, not even seductive San Francisco. He hadn't traveled this far, to what he called "the wild side of the continent," to find commercialism and hives of men droning after dollars. The East was already full of that. This man's wealth dwelled elsewhere: in the mountains, the forests, the great cathedrals of nature that filled him with peace.

For several years he had vacillated between his two great loves: nature and inventing; he had a remarkable penchant for both. "If you walk the fields with him," an admirer once wrote of Muir, "you will find that Solomon could not speak more wisely about plants."

While nature called him outside, inventing kept him in. "I was in great danger of becoming so successful," he said of his experiments with machinery, "that my botanical and geographical studies might be interrupted."

Fate made the decision for him.

A year before landing in California, he was working in an Indianapolis carriage factory when a metal file slipped from his grip and flew into the cornea of his right eye. The eye's aqueous humor fell into his cupped hand. He walked to a window and saw nothing. "My right eye gone," he lamented quietly. "Closed forever on all God's beauty." Soon his other eye went blind from sympathetic nervous shock. Bedridden in a dark room, he prayed for a miracle to give back his vision. And he vowed that he would follow nature and dedicate his life to it. The miracle arrived.

With his sight restored, he walked a thousand miles to Florida "by the wildest, leafiest, and least trodden way." En route and penniless in Savannah, he slept in a cemetery until his brother sent him money; then he feasted on gingerbread. After visiting Florida and Cuba, he boarded a ship west.

*Turbulent sunset sky dwarfs Half Dome, the great granite landmark of Yosemite Valley.*

*PRECEDING PAGES: Sculpted and polished by glaciers thousands of years ago, Liberty Cap rises above 594-foot Nevada Fall on the Merced River in California's Yosemite National Park.*

Thus John Muir, son of the wilderness, one month shy of 30 and still at the trailhead of his life, arrived in California.

He walked to the Sierra Nevada—what he called "The Range of Light"—and into the grandeur of Yosemite, where his name and values would be enshrined forever.

"Climb the mountains and get their good tidings," he exulted. "Nature's peace will flow into you as sunshine flows into trees. The winds will blow their own freshness into you, and the storms their energy, while cares will drop off like autumn leaves."

Off he'd go, up before the sun, hiking free, climbing high, his feet skipping over the granite, his senses alert to every rock, flower, birdsong, and stream. No time to boil tea; just chew on the leaves. A couple of pieces of bread or oatmeal sufficed for lunch and dinner. It wasn't food that sustained him, after all, but wildness: the mountains, meadows, and forests he believed were God's true temples, the best "conductor of divinity."

His father, a strict Calvinist, never fully understood him. Neither did others of rigid and narrow orthodoxies. Young John had refused to patent his inventions, believing "all improvements…should be the property of the human race." Perhaps it was his Highland blood that pulled him into the mountains; he'd been born in Scotland and lived there his first 11 years, before his family sailed to America and settled in Wisconsin. From nature he learned the lessons of cooperation, not competition, and saw the daily struggles of the common man as sadly cruel, exploitative, and utilitarian. Laissez-faire was the doctrine of the day, with every man for himself. Muir shook his head and called it "the gobble gobble school of economics."

Yosemite was his cathedral and university, its great granite walls streaked with ribbonlike waterfalls, its mountain streams alive with water ouzels, its meadows painted by exquisite parades of wildflowers: what better place for a quintessential self-taught naturalist, one too restless for the stuffy halls of formal academia. He would take his lessons and inspiration from the seasons, from thousands of days and hundreds of adventures in the unmapped contours of California. In time, like the seedling of a sequoia, he would grow to great heights, his inquisitive spirit branching into every facet of natural history around him.

He determined from the subtle signatures of ice—striations in granite, valley floor moraines, concentric rock cleavages—that Yosemite Valley had been excavated by glaciers and was not the product of primal cataclysm, as Josiah D. Whitney, state geologist of California and professor of geology at Harvard, had proclaimed. Whitney was indignant. Who was this "mere sheepherder" and "ignoramus" who dared to challenge his scientific authority?

"A physical fact is as sacred as a moral principle," Muir responded. "I can take you where you can see for yourself how the glaciers have labored, and cut and carved, and elaborated, until they have wrought out this royal road." This Yosemite Valley, a Pleistocene temple built by ice.

California newspapers carried the debate, and people began to talk about John Muir.

More visitors arrived, among them Joseph Le Conte, professor of geology at the University of California, who recognized the genius of Muir's theory, and sided with him. Then came Thérèse Yelverton, an erstwhile lady-in-waiting to European royalty who had traveled to America to write books and articles. In John Muir she found a charming Yosemite guide and a perfect protagonist for her next novel. She asked him to travel with her. But Muir belonged to the mountains, and the lady eventually sailed to the Orient alone. "At this period and for some years to come," wrote a Muir biographer, Linnie Marsh Wolfe, "his all-consuming passion for the wilderness lay like a sword between himself and love for any woman."

The following spring, May 1871, Ralph Waldo Emerson, the famous essayist and poet, came to Yosemite. Muir had read his writings and was eager to met him, for Emerson was the Wise Man of the East, the New England transcendentalist who'd written: "The earth laughs in flowers" and "If a single man plant himself indomitably on his instincts, and there abide, the huge world will come round to him." Nearly 70 and somewhat infirm, Emerson retained a mind as sharp as ever. Riding a pied mustang through Yosemite Valley, he gazed up at sunshine dancing off granite spires and commented, "This valley is the only place that comes up to the brag about it, and exceeds it."

Others in Emerson's Eastern entourage discussed Dante, Michelangelo, Ruppini, and Machiavelli with such incessant, bookish fervor that the sublime music of Yosemite—the songs of water, wind, and wildlife—escaped them. Emerson, too, had brought his purple bag of books, but observers say he didn't read them. Instead, he listened. He looked. He spent long hours on the hotel veranda, welcoming those who came calling. John Muir, bashful in his miller's garb and untrimmed beard, stood in the background and declined to come forward. But Emerson had received a note from a friend telling him that if he could meet only one person in Yosemite, make it the young Scotsman named Muir.

So the following morning the saintly old man slipped away from his Bostonian acolytes and rode his mustang over to the mill where Muir worked. Their meeting was magical. Muir's shyness evaporated as he spread his treasures before the regal older man: rocks; plant specimens; sketches of glaciers, peaks, and forests; diagrams on the patterns and processes of nature—all offered with zeal. Emerson was charmed. They spoke for hours.

"I proposed an immeasurable camping trip back in the heart of the mountains," Muir said, "But alas, it was too late, —too near the sundown of his [Emerson's] life. The shadows were growing long, and he leaned on his friends. His party, full of indoor philosophy, failed to see the natural beauty…of my wild plan, and laughed at it….Anyhow, they would have none of it, and held Mr. Emerson to the hotels and trails."

The following days found them increasingly inseparable, Muir and Emerson, Western prodigy and Eastern mentor, speaking their intimate language of appreciation for the natural world. Emerson asked his young friend to depart the valley with him, so they might ride a day or two together. Muir accepted, and on a ridge above a forest he commented on how the sugar pines spread "their arms with majestic gestures, addressing the surrounding trees like very priests of the woods." Emerson, pondering this, said surely no forest had "so fine a preacher or so well-dressed and well-behaved and devout a congregation."

While the rest of the party quoted obtuse passages from Sir Walter Scott, Muir and Emerson sat in silent communion beneath the big trees.

Again Muir suggested a camp-out in the woods, and again he was rebuffed by the others who insisted Mr. Emerson stay in a nearby hostelry,

"Everybody needs beauty as well as bread, places to play in and pray in, where Nature may heal and cheer and give strength...."

—JOHN MUIR
*THE MOUNTAINS OF CALIFORNIA*

with what Muir called "carpet dust and unknowable reeks."

The next morning they parted, each waving to the other until out of sight. John Muir would later recall the two supreme moments of his life as finding a calypso blooming alone in a Canadian bog and meeting Emerson. Years after Emerson died, a short list of great names entitled "My Men" was found in his journals. They were the luminaries who had inspired him. The last name added was that of John Muir.

To fully understand a portrait of these two men, consider the America in which they were framed. Not for another hundred years would there be an Earth Day or an Endangered Species Act. The common vocabulary would become salted with terms like "ecology," "environment," "ecosystem," "wetland," "habitat," and "biosphere." At the time Muir and Emerson met, 1871, America was still a place for the taking, not the saving. To attain the good life was to harness every resource. Level the forests. Plow the land. Fence the fields. The pursuit of material progress brooked no tolerance for wilderness, which was an obstacle at best, an evil at worst, the physical and spiritual enemy of paradise. Men were called upon to convert the wild into the pastoral, for God would comfort Zion, as the Bible promised, and "make her wilderness like Eden." Providence had obviously hidden this vast and bountiful continent for centuries, the new settlers believed, so they could now do his work. This was the American birthmark: new people, old values, raw land.

The Pilgrims who landed at Plymouth Rock in 1620 were English separatists in search of religious and political freedoms. Oliver Cromwell's thugs might terrorize nearby Ireland, but not faraway America. Here pioneers would find another world, a sanctuary that was utterly wild, but one nonetheless rich in what historian Daniel Boorstin called "the therapy of distance....[where] the tradition of self government, which had been established in England by the weight of hundreds of years, was being established in America by the force of hundreds of miles."

The immediate challenge was survival. The Pilgrims stood on the threshold of the unknown, with the sea to their backs and the wilderness ahead— a perilous place that was anything but the tonic John Muir would proclaim it to be a quarter of a millennium later. It was an alien element filled with demons, savages, and dark spirits. It swallowed children who entered it unprepared. It magnified fears. "What could they see but a hideous and desolate wilderness," wrote William Bradford in 1620, "full of wild beasts and wild men? And what multitudes there might be of them they knew not."

"Wilderness" and "bewilder," offspring of the same root, would form an unbroken bond in the American psyche for hundreds of years. What better source of pride for a frontiersman than to subjugate the wilderness. Ax and plow were his instruments of virtue. As the forests fell, tendrils of civilization reached up and down the eastern seaboard, along rivers and over mountains. Commerce expanded. Cities were born.

It is ironic that urbanites with their pens, not pioneers with their plows, were the first to express an appreciation for wilderness. As Romanticism flowered in 18th-century Europe, so did an enlightened view of wild country. Primitivists like Jean-Jacques Rousseau warned of the creeping decadence of crowded, insipid societies. Poets in England condemned "smoky cities" and pined for the purity of the "pathless wilds." In his memorable story of Robinson Crusoe, published in 1719 to a wide audience, Daniel

"Nature streaming into us, wooingly teaching her wonderful glowing lessons... every wild lesson a love lesson...."

—JOHN MUIR
*THE STORY OF MY BOYHOOD AND YOUTH*

Defoe described the magic to be found in solitude and nature, implying sharp contrasts to civilization's clutter and artifice.

A few educated Europeans became so intrigued with wild America that they traveled here to taste it firsthand. When François-René de Chateaubriand visited northern New York in the winter of 1791-92, he described his "sort of delirium" with the absence of roads and royalty: "…in this deserted region the soul delights to bury and lose itself amidst boundless forests…to mix and confound…with the wild sublimities of Nature."

Alexis de Tocqueville and Lord Byron echoed de Chateaubriand's sentiments, but avaricious Americans were slow to awaken to the natural treasures around them. "Democratic nations," wrote de Tocqueville, "will habitually prefer the useful to the beautiful, and they will require that the beautiful should be useful."

The American pioneer had his paradox, and so destroyed the anvil on which he was forged: wilderness. In 1810, 76-year-old Daniel Boone lamented to 25-year-old John James Audubon: "Why, at the time when I was caught by the Indians [30 years earlier], you would not have walked out in any direction for more than a mile without shooting a buck or a bear. There were then thousands of buffaloes on the hills in Kentucky; the land looked as if it would never become poor; and the hunt in those days was a pleasure indeed. But when I was left to myself on the banks of the Green River, I daresay for the last time in my life, a few signs only of deer were to be seen, and, as to a deer itself, I saw none."

Years later, as he traveled through the Ohio River Valley, Audubon would see for himself the destructive power of the pioneer. "The greedy mills," he wrote, "told the sad tale, that in a century the noble forests…should exist no more." Other artists and naturalists—notably George Catlin, who pondered the idea of national parks as early as 1832—shared Audubon's concerns.

The assumption of natural resource inexhaustibleness was a recurring theme in the settlement of wild America. Some said it would take a thousand years to pioneer and populate the continent. It in fact took less than a hundred. By 1811 the Pacific Fur Company arrived on the Oregon Coast, and in 1812 Wyoming's South Pass, the best route over the Rocky Mountains, was discovered. The war of western acquisition would soon begin, fulfilling shamans' dark dreams of flooding tides of white men and the end of the Indian way of life. Barbed wire would replace buffalo. Little Big Horn would be followed by the massacre at Wounded Knee.

So vast, strange, and magnificent was the American landscape that many men and women who settled it became players in their own mythologies. Jim Bridger, Kit Carson, Zebulon Pike, and John C. Frémont—first candidate for President on the Republican ticket—were heroes who shaped, and were shaped by, the American West. The doctrine of Manifest Destiny said it was not only their right but their duty to expand from sea to sea and make the United States a single great continent-nation.

Yet as this juggernaut of growth and expansion marched west, dissenting voices could be heard in the East. James Fenimore Cooper created Natty Bumppo, or Leatherstocking, his most popular character, who found in the wilderness not an adversary to be vanquished but a deep moral influence in "the honesty of the woods." Painter Thomas Cole depicted what he called "the wild and great features of nature: mountainous forests that know not

*FOLLOWING PAGES: A Steller's jay perches in a frosted willow. Named for German naturalist Georg Wilhelm Steller, who accompanied Vitus Bering in his discovery of Alaska in 1741, this jay convinced Steller, who had never seen one in Europe or Asia, that he and Bering had indeed landed in the New World, not the Old.*

MICHAEL FRYE

man." In 1836 he wrote: "American scenery...has features, and glorious ones, unknown to Europe...the most distinctive, and perhaps the most impressive, characteristic of American scenery is its wildness."

Emerson concurred, writing in the same year, "Nature is the symbol of the spirit."

A celebration of wild America thus began. Would it be too late?

In 1837, the year before John Muir's birth, a 19-year-old Harvard graduate with fine features and soulful eyes spoke at his commencement ceremony and warned of the commercial, viruslike spirit infecting New England. His classmates hardly agreed; they had careers to pursue and loans to liquidate. They would follow their own paths; the young speaker, his. He was Henry David Thoreau, the son of a pencil manufacturer and a friend of Emerson, who would never marry or hold a steady job but who, in his 44 short years, would become a Mozart and a Michelangelo in expressing an enlightened view of nature.

In 1845 he moved to Walden Pond, near his home in Concord, Massachusetts, and built a cabin that would contain a table, a low cot, a slant-top desk, and three chairs—"one for solitude, two for friendship, three for society."

He stayed for a little more than two years, and though he made frequent visits to town, he was always most eager to return to the solitude of Walden.

"I went to the woods because I wished to live deliberately," he wrote, "to front only the essential facts of life, and see if I could not learn what it had to teach, and not, when I came to die, discover that I had not lived."

Like Emerson and a handful of others at the time, Thoreau was a transcendentalist who believed natural objects, when rightly seen, reflected universal spiritual truths. If men would stop swinging their hammers and counting their ledgers long enough to transcend themselves as he had done, rising from the rational to the intuitive, from the banal to the imaginative, they would discover the divine in the vein of a leaf, the beauty in the flight of a butterfly, the perfection in the song of a thrush.

"Why level downward to our dullest perception always," he asked, "and praise that as common sense? The commonest sense is the sense of men asleep, which they express by snoring."

Describing Thoreau in NATIONAL GEOGRAPHIC magazine (March 1981), Princeton professor William Howarth wrote: "He dressed for his walks like a common laborer, the only college graduate in town to wear a muslin shirt, corduroy pants, and unpolished shoes with pegged soles. He carried a notched stick for measurements and a spyglass for birds. In his straw hat was a scaffold lining, where he could store plants. Humid 'vapors' from his head made the hat a perfect 'botany-box,' he claimed."

Villagers thought Walden Pond was bottomless, but Thoreau knew otherwise: By drawing lines between the points of greatest width and length, he found the pond's maximum depth—102 feet—to be precisely where the two lines intersected. Alas, he decided, the pond might appear random on the surface, but hidden below was elegance and symmetry.

Could this be a metaphor of his fellowman? "Perhaps we need only to know how his shores trend and his adjacent country or circumstances, to infer his depth and concealed bottom."

He shared his observations with friends and their children, but typically walked alone in the woods, at times crawling on hands and knees to better see mosses, lichens, and flowers. He would splash through creeks and brooks, sometimes wearing only his hat and shirt, then sun himself on a rock, deep in his own thoughts, silently writing in his journal.

"I would rather sit on a pumpkin and have it all to myself, than be crowded on a velvet cushion."

Midway through his time at Walden, in 1846, he went to jail for one night for refusing to pay a poll tax because his government not only condoned slavery, but was at war with Mexico. Aghast, Emerson visited his friend and asked what on earth he was doing "in there?" Thoreau, equally disturbed that his elder colleague, a man of letters, had not properly searched his own conscience, asked Emerson what he was doing "out there?"

In his essay, "Civil Disobedience," published in 1849, Thoreau recalled: "I was put into a jail...and, as I stood considering the walls of solid stone, two or three feet thick, the door of wood and iron, a foot thick, and the iron grating which strained the light, I could not help being struck with the foolishness of that institution which treated me as if I were mere flesh and blood and bones, to be locked up.... The State never intentionally confronts a man's sense, intellectual or moral, but only his body, his senses."

His words would circle the world. Among those who would find them inspirational: Leo Tolstoy, Mahatma Gandhi, and Martin Luther King.

Just as men waged war on each other, Thoreau believed they waged it on the natural world. As he observed in his masterpiece, *Walden*, published in 1854: "Why should we be in such desperate haste to succeed and in such desperate enterprises? If a man does not keep pace with his companions, perhaps it is because he hears a different drummer. Let him step to the music which he hears, however measured or far away."

He knew he was critically ill when he journeyed west to the Great Lakes in 1861. But as a student of history, nature, and culture he was compelled to go, and so implored others, "Be...the Lewis and Clark and Frobisher, of your own streams and oceans; explore your own higher latitudes....Be a Columbus to whole new continents and worlds within you, opening new channels, not of trade, but of thought. Every man is the lord of a realm beside which the earthly empire of the Czar is but a petty state, a hummock left by the ice."

At Thoreau's deathbed back in Concord, someone asked Thoreau if he had made his peace with God, to which the sick man replied, "I did not know that we had ever quarreled."

It should be no surprise that among the ideas John Muir carried with him into Yosemite six years after Thoreau died were those born in *Walden*.

"Muir was himself an original," wrote Linnie Marsh Wolfe. "He was never warped out of his own orbit or made a satellite to any man or system of thinking. But he was hospitable to Emerson's ideas because like cleavage planes in rocks, awaiting development, they were indigenous within himself. When Emerson said: 'Every rational creature has in Nature a dowry and estate. It is his if he will,' the words struck like fire in Muir's mind. Remembering them, in due time he went out to claim his dowry and to reject all compromises. The gentle Emerson, happy in his Concord meadows, never wholly took possession of his estate. Like Moses, he only pointed the way. Thoreau and Muir alone of all his followers fully *lived* His nature gospel."

"Every morning was a cheerful invitation to make my life of equal simplicity, and I may say innocence, with Nature herself."

—HENRY DAVID THOREAU
*WALDEN*

Others were not far behind. While Muir and Emerson shared precious hours in Yosemite in 1871, another notable chapter in American conservation was unfolding some 700 miles to the northeast, in Yellowstone, heart of the Rocky Mountains. Ferdinand V. Hayden, director of the Geological and Geographical Survey of the Territories of the American West, visited the area with landscape artist Thomas Moran and photographer William Henry Jackson. What they recorded was no less fantastic than the stories preserved from a year before when a 19-man expedition had spent more than a month wandering through the fabled land of geysers, hot springs, canyons, waterfalls, and wolf howls.

Just as Alice had had her Wonderland, these men had their Yellowstone. Sitting around a campfire one chilled September night, they discussed the future of the area. Most said they intended to file claims in anticipation of the tourist trade, sure to come. Two men dissented. Cornelius Hedges and Nathaniel P. Langford, transplanted Easterners in Montana, said Yellowstone deserved better. Must every American icon be defaced by commercial development? they asked. Here was a chance to follow the moral higher ground, to forsake avarice and save wild nature, as George Catlin had said nearly 40 years earlier, as "a magnificent park.… What a beautiful and thrilling specimen for America to preserve and hold up to the view of her refined citizens and the world, in future ages."

Hayden and his party agreed, and returned East to a receptive audience. "There is something romantic in the thought," gushed the *New York Times,* "that, in spite of the restless activity of our people, and the almost fabulous rapidity of their increase, vast tracts of national domain yet remain unexplored."

Inspired by the lectures and writings of Langford and the photographs of Jackson, Congress tackled the issue, and on March 1, 1872, President Grant signed a bill creating "a public park or pleasuring ground" called Yellowstone. The world had its first national park—an idea every bit as American as democracy, bluegrass music, and apple pie.

No sooner was it established than it was challenged. The powerful railroads wanted the park to be a collection of natural curiosities to attract passengers but not an extensive wilderness that would hamstring rights-of-way for mining and timber extractions. A sympathetic senator berated the federal government for entering "show business" with the park, but was quickly upbraided by another senator, George G. Vest of Missouri, who in the tradition of the transcendentalists replied that America needed Yellowstone "as a great breathing-place for the national lungs."

The House of Representatives also debated the railroad issue. "I can not understand the sentiment," said one frustrated congressman, "which favors the retention of a few buffaloes to the development of mining interests amounting to millions of dollars." William McAdoo of New Jersey urged the understanding that Yellowstone was created for people now and forever who will discover "in the great West the inspiring sights and mysteries of nature that elevate mankind and bring it closer communion with omniscience."

Congress voted. The railroads lost. For the first time in American history, in 1886—four years after Emerson died and the West's last great buffalo herd was slaughtered by long-rifled sharpshooters—powerful promoters of wilderness and commerce came eye-to-eye.

And commerce blinked.

Shortly before, in August 1885, John Muir had visited Yellowstone en route to Wisconsin to see his brothers and sisters and his ailing father. John himself was not well, and his wife knew it. He wrote to her in California of this "strange region of fire and water," lamenting that he wished he had more time to explore its wonders.

"Oh, if you could only feel unhurried and able to rest with no thought of tomorrow, next week, or next month," she responded. "There must be the charm of healing in your own high wilderness. Only one week in the Rocky Mountain wilderness for John Muir! Oh, my beloved, you are cruel to yourself."

After five years of marriage, Mrs. Louie Strenzel Muir understood—or was beginning to understand—the full importance of wilderness in her husband's life. A quiet woman with gray eyes and raven hair, she could have been a concert pianist and traveled to the great cities of the world. She chose the country life instead. Fame didn't appeal to her. Her father was a leading California horticulturist, and she had had many suitors, none of whom mattered after the summer of 1874 when she had met John Muir and had confided in her diary: "How I should love to become acquainted with a person who writes as he does. What is wealth compared to a mind like his!"

They had been married in April 1880, six months after John had made his first epic journey to Alaska and found Glacier Bay. Paddling a canoe into the iceberg-filled waters with four Tlingit and a Presbyterian minister, he had sat in the bow and had been hardly able to contain his excitement. There was a bay rich with tidewater glaciers flowing from the mountains into the sea, a landscape still locked in the Pleistocene where he could prove his theories of glaciation in Yosemite. There was ancient ice, he had written, "broken into an imposing array of jagged spires and pyramids, and flat-topped towers and battlements, of many shades of blue, from pale, shimmering, limpid tones in the crevasses and hollows, to the most startling, chilling, almost shrieking vitriol blue on the plain mural spaces from which bergs had just been discharged."

The Tlingit, nearly mutinous in the cold and rain, had asked: Why does Muir climb mountains in gathering storms?

To gain knowledge, the minister had replied.

The Tlingit had recited melancholy stories of relatives lost in ice-crushed canoes and sudden snows. They had said, "Muir must be a witch to seek knowledge in such a place as this and in such miserable weather."

But Muir, returning "wet and weary and glad," had rallied the sour men with his infectious glee and later had described Glacier Bay as an "icy wildness unspeakably pure and sublime."

Since that time, marriage and time on the ranch—what Muir called "this humdrum, work-a-day life"—had domesticated him into a malaise. Even though Louie was pregnant with their second daughter in this summer of 1885, she knew she must release her husband from constant ranch life to renew his spirit. He would never forsake his family, devoted as he was, but neither must he forsake the mountains, forests, and flowers that gifted him with the voice she loved.

So John Muir returned to his Yosemite, and Alaska. He also climbed Mount Rainier and upon returning to Seattle received a letter from Louie:

"I am hopelessly and forever a mountaineer. ...and I care to live only to entice people to look at Nature's loveliness."

—JOHN MUIR
*LETTER, OCTOBER 1874*

"The Alaska book and the Yosemite book, dear John, must be written, and you need to be your own self, well and strong, to make them worthy of you. There is nothing that has a right to be considered beside this except the welfare of our children."

He was free, and being free he picked up the banner of wilderness to become a crusader. Disgusted with lumbermen who cut down sequoias, he wrote: "It took more than three thousand years to make some of the trees in these Western woods—trees that are still standing in perfect strength and beauty, waving and singing in the mighty forests of the Sierra. Through all the wonderful, eventful centuries since Christ's time—and long before that—God had cared for these trees, saved them from drought, disease, avalanches, and a thousand straining, leveling tempests and floods; but he cannot save them from fools...."

In 1892 he founded the Sierra Club, just in time to defeat a congressional bill that called for cutting down half the trees in Yosemite. The following year found him in Chicago, en route to New York, where he would meet Mark Twain and Rudyard Kipling before crossing the Atlantic to visit Europe and his native Scotland. Chicago was host of the World's Fair that year, but Muir found it "a cosmopolitan rat's nest" and quickly departed. Had he lingered, however, he might have heard a speech that would have fascinated him, perhaps even haunted him.

Delivered to the American Historical Association by a young historian and fellow Wisconsinite named Frederick Jackson Turner, it was entitled "The Significance of the Frontier in American History." Prior to Turner's speech, most historians believed America had been defined first by distancing itself from European influences and second by surviving the Civil War. Turner offered a third theory, challenging the prevailing order, as great theorists must do, by saying the frontier more than anything else is what made Americans unique. And what will happen to the American spirit, he asked, now that the frontier is gone? Indeed, the superintendent of the United States Census had recorded the national population and produced a map delineating the American frontier, which had retreated steadily westward before the quenchless thirst of white settlers. The 1890 map was significant, Turner said, because it showed no frontier at all. It had disappeared.

Would the best of America disappear with it? he asked. "That coarseness and strength combined with acuteness and inquisitiveness; that practical, inventive turn of mind, quick to find expedients; that masterful grasp of material things, lacking in the artistic but powerful to affect great ends; that restless, nervous energy; that dominant individualism, working for good and evil, and withal the buoyancy and exuberance which comes with freedom—these are the traits of the frontier, or traits called out elsewhere because of the existence of the frontier."

Certainly they would not die, but neither would they remain the same. In destroying her own frontier, America had unwittingly made herself more like Europe: a latter-day domesticated continent with shrinking vestiges of a wild youth.

People in larger numbers began to believe Thoreau had been right when in 1861 he wrote, "In Wildness is the preservation of the World."

During his travels to the East and Europe in 1893, John Muir stopped at Walden Pond and visited the old cabin site of that "blessed crank and tramp." How his heart must have soared on hallowed ground where today thousands of weekend swimmers enjoy the beaches. Civilization is crowding Walden Pond, yet recent attempts by developers to build nearby condominiums and shopping malls have been rebuffed by growing legions of Thoreauvians, young and old, who refuse to tolerate such desecrations. Likewise, across the continent growing public sentiment demands that the National Park Service remove more and more traffic, commercialism, and human clutter from Muir's sacred Yosemite Valley.

Neither man, Thoreau nor Muir, could have foreseen the stature America would someday accord him. Each met serious opposition in his day, but neither flagged in his vision or voice. "To be great is to be misunderstood," Emerson had said. The understanding would come later.

In 1903, when President Theodore Roosevelt went to visit Yosemite, he, like Emerson, was attended by a flock of fawning sycophants. Yet unlike Emerson, Roosevelt was determined to camp. An outdoorsman himself, he began talking about shooting game, to which Muir, who stood in the shadow of no man, asked, "Mr. Roosevelt, when are you going to get beyond the boyishness of killing things…? Are you not getting far enough along to leave that off?"

The sycophants nearly fell over.

Roosevelt replied, "Muir, I guess you're right."

He would go hunting nonetheless, but for museum specimens, he explained, not for sport. "Bully," he exclaimed many times as he admired the grandeur around him. He and Muir camped one night on Glacier Point, high above the valley floor, and awoke the next morning in four inches of new snow. "This is bullier yet," T. R. howled. "I wouldn't miss this for anything."

As they stood together on the point—Muir, the bearded crusader, and Roosevelt, the effervescent president 20 years Muir's junior—they watched two great dawnings: one of rose quartz alpenglow on the High Sierra, the other of a new promise in a new century for wilderness in America. Muir spoke of "timber thieves" and "spoilers of the forests" while T. R. listened. That same year back in Washington he would create the first federal wildlife refuge and begin a habitat and wildlife protection system that would someday total hundreds of millions of acres. Every year thereafter great strides would be taken to save wild America, yet great losses would continue as well. The preservation race was on.

John Muir had entered the Sierra 35 years earlier and had seen many changes. Some would say the biggest change of all, the one yet to come—the damming of Hetch Hetchy Valley, comparable to flooding Yosemite Valley—would break his heart and be responsible for his death on Christmas Eve 1914. Roosevelt would grudgingly approve of the dam. Yet it is said that Muir forgave him. They had camped together in the snow, after all. When you find a heaven on earth, as Muir had found in the mountains and forests of wild America, it is easy to forgive.

"How deep our sleep last night in the mountain's heart," he wrote in *My First Summer in the Sierra,* "beneath the trees and stars, hushed by solemn-sounding waterfalls and many small soothing voices in sweet accord, whispering peace."

In seeking the prophecies of nature, John Muir, like Henry David Thoreau, had himself become a prophet.

"The battle for conservation will go on endlessly. It is part of the universal warfare between right and wrong."

—JOHN MUIR

# "Mountain parks...are useful not only as fountains of timber and irrigating rivers, but as fountains of life."

—JOHN MUIR, *OUR NATIONAL PARKS*

*Wisps of a clearing storm veil the cliffs of Glacier Point in California's Yosemite Valley.*
*If "the earth laughs in flowers," as Ralph Waldo Emerson said, this camas caked in morning frost smiles.*

*PRECEDING PAGES: Running free, as John Muir believed all rivers should, the Tuolumne flows through the Yosemite high country with Unicorn Peak in the background.*

*The dean of 19th-century American wildlife painters, John James Audubon captured on canvas the color and vitality of many birds, some that now no longer exist. He lamented that [Carolina] parakeets (below, left) "are destroyed in great numbers...." Of passenger pigeons (below, right), which numbered more than a billion in 1813, he observed as they flew overhead: "The light of noon-day was obscured as by an eclipse." A century later the species was extinct. Two female white phase gyrfalcons (opposite) impressed the naturalist, as he noted, "I saw these warriors descend like a streak of lightning."*

PAINTINGS BY JOHN JAMES AUDUBON, COLLECTION OF THE NEW-YORK HISTORICAL SOCIETY

"Parakeets are destroyed in great numbers.... Ten, or even twenty, are killed at every discharge."

—JOHN JAMES AUDUBON
*ORNITHOLOGICAL BIOGRAPHY*

"A lake is the landscape's most beautiful and expressive feature."

—HENRY DAVID THOREAU
*WALDEN*

*A*utumn reflections
*enliven the waters
of Walden Pond,
near Concord,
Massachusetts, where
transcendentalist
Henry David Thoreau
lived in a simple cabin
from July 1845
to September 1847.
"It is a clear and deep
green well," he wrote,
an ideal place to fill his
journal, play his flute,
and fish by midnight
moonlight, "serenaded
by owls and foxes, and
hearing, from time to
time, the creaking note
of some unknown
bird close at hand."*

*FOLLOWING PAGES:
A stately sugar maple
becomes an autumn
palette in Vermont's
Green Mountain
National Forest.*

*Cinnabar light anoints autumn woods in Baxter State Park, beneath storm clouds and Mount Katahdin, at 5,267 feet, the highest point in Maine. Former governor Percival Baxter acquired more than 200,000 acres of northern Maine wilderness*

and donated it to the state. Along with Henry David Thoreau, Robert Marshall, and other visionaries, Baxter had found challenge and inspiration in these Maine woods, which remain today a final bastion of primordial eastern American forest.

*A* lichen-covered rock and reflective pond in New Hampshire's White Mountain
National Forest display autumn maple leaves. "It is the marriage of the soul
with Nature that makes the intellect fruitful, and gives birth to imagination,"
wrote Henry David Thoreau, who reveled in such quiet places.
The ivory-like waters of Moss Glenn Falls (above) cascade past a red maple beginning
to turn color in September, in Green Mountain National Forest, Vermont.

FOLLOWING PAGES: Calved from a nearby tidewater glacier, icebergs lie stranded
at low tide along the shore of Muir Inlet, glittering like diamonds in the setting sun in
Alaska's Glacier Bay National Park. For thousands of years this entire landscape—
the bay, the inlet, the surrounding mountains—lay buried beneath Muir Glacier, which
retreated roughly 70 miles from the 1790s to the 1980s.

> "The grandeur of these forces and their glorious results overpower me....In dreams I read blurred sheets of glacial writing...."
>
> —JOHN MUIR

*A*long *Glacier Bay strawberry leaves and pioneering lichen brighten glacier-polished white marble (above), while a June morning finds yellow cinquefoil flowers (right), members of the rose family, mingling with a young Sitka spruce, the state tree of Alaska.*

*FOLLOWING PAGES: "The clouds began to rise from the lower altitudes," wrote John Muir of Glacier Bay, "slowly lifting their white skirts, and lingering in majestic, wing-shaped masses about the mountains that rise out of the broad, icy sea, the highest of all the white mountains, and the greatest of all the glaciers I had yet seen."*

# THINKING LIKE
# A MOUNTAIN

# Aldo Leopold and the Land Ethic

"We were eating lunch on a high rimrock, at the foot of which a turbulent river elbowed its way," wrote Aldo Leopold in his essay, "Thinking Like a Mountain."

ALDO LEOPOLD

He and fellow foresters were in the Blue Range of Arizona's Apache National Forest, sowing wild oats and embracing their tenets of wildlife management—still framed in frontier myths—when they saw a deer far below. They watched it cross the river, belly-deep in white water, emerge on the near bank, and shake itself dry. That's when they realized it wasn't a deer at all, but a mother wolf. Half a dozen grown pups burst from a willow thicket to greet her, frisking and wagging their tails. Leopold, 22 years old and fresh out of Yale Forest School, grabbed his rifle. So did the others.

The year was 1909.

"In those days we had never heard of passing up a chance to kill a wolf," he remembered. They fired into the family "with more excitement than accuracy....When our rifles were empty, the old wolf was down, and a pup was dragging a leg into impassable slide-rocks.

"We reached the old wolf in time to watch a fierce green fire dying in her eyes; I realized then, and have known ever since, that there was something new to me in those eyes—something known only to her and to the mountain. I was young then, and full of trigger itch; I thought that because fewer wolves meant more deer, that no wolves would mean hunters' paradise. But after seeing the green fire die, I sensed that neither the wolf nor the mountain agreed with such a view."

Every life has its epiphanies, those wondrous moments that flash new worlds across the imagination. For Aldo Leopold—forester, naturalist, hunter—no such moments went unharnessed; he learned from them all and grew well beyond common horizons. The forester became a professor; the naturalist, a philosopher; the hunter, a co-founder of the modern sciences of ecology and wildlife management. And more; no boundary contained him. With profound powers of observation, a rational mind, and

*Whitetail doe and fawn find refuge in Aldo Leopold's land ethic, which enlarges the biological community to include soils, water, plants, and animals.*

*PRECEDING PAGES: McKnight Mountain looks toward the Black Range in the Aldo Leopold Wilderness Area, in New Mexico's Gila National Forest.*

a gift for eloquence, Aldo Leopold would grow to redefine relationships between farmer and field, forester and forests, hunter and hunted. He would recognize human and natural history as twin pillars of the same edifice, a double helix of the same organism, inextricably woven together and destined either to thrive in harmony or to decay in discordance.

Our relationship with the earth, he said, must be like our relationship with one another—a product of social evolution, a ceaseless exercise in respect. The land is not a commodity, but a community—a complex yet lovely aggregate of living beings interactive with, and dependent upon, each other. Forsake this community, and we forsake the better part of ourselves; we become as sterile as the land we abuse. "It is a matter of what a man thinks about while chopping, or while deciding what to chop," he pondered. "A conservationist is one who is humbly aware that with each stroke he is writing his signature on the face of his land."

This was Leopold's genius: what he called "ecological conscience" and "the land ethic." "I have lived to see state after state extirpate its wolves," he wrote long after the incident on the Apache rimrock. "I have watched the face of many a newly wolfless mountain, and seen the south-facing slopes wrinkle with a maze of new deer trails."

With the predators gone, so, too, was the natural balance. The deer consumed every eatable seedling, shrub, and flower, every sprig, shoot, and bud. Their numbers exploded, then crashed. Mass starvation littered their bones and carcasses amid the pauperized mountainsides of their own destruction, none of it a mystery to the older, enlightened Leopold.

"I now suspect that just as a deer herd lives in mortal fear of its wolves, so does a mountain live in mortal fear of its deer. And perhaps with better cause, for while a buck pulled down by wolves can be replaced in two or three years, a range pulled down by too many deer may fail of replacement in as many decades."

Leopold lamented the loss of wild America, but he didn't despair. He explored the restorative powers of nature as he did the learning curves of men, most intensely his own. He wondered: Is it our pursuit of safety and prosperity, our near-neurotic obsession with security, that distances us from the natural world? "A measure of success in this is all well enough, and perhaps is a requisite to objective thinking, but too much safety seems to yield only danger in the long run. Perhaps this is behind Thoreau's dictum: In wildness is the salvation of the world. Perhaps this is the hidden meaning in the howl of the wolf, long known among mountains, but seldom perceived among men."

The longest war of all, Leopold knew, was that of man against nature.

On a fine spring day nearly 40 years after seeing the fierce green fire die, he was planting pines and counting geese on his property on a bend of the Wisconsin River, a short distance north of Madison, with his beloved wife, Estella, and the youngest of their five children, "Estella Jr." It was April 21, 1948, the birthday of John Muir, a son of the wilderness and founder of the Sierra Club. Muir, cut from the same conservation cloth as Leopold, had been born 110 years earlier in Scotland and had been reared on a farm not far away in south-central Wisconsin.

Only six weeks before, in early March, Leopold had written the final words of *A Sand County Almanac,* his collection of observations and essays (including "Thinking Like A Mountain") that would become his greatest work, still widely read some 50 years after its first publication.

Yet he would witness none of it.

About midmorning he and his two Estellas saw smoke rising to the east. A neighbor's trash fire had escaped, and the wind was raking the flames across a marsh toward the Leopold pines and the chicken coop the family had renovated into a cozy weekend retreat they endearingly called "the shack." They quickly loaded their car with fire-fighting equipment— a shovel, a small hand-held fire pump, gunny sacks—and raced down the road. Leopold had met everything else in his life head-on; this fire would be no different. He instructed his wife to wait by the car and his daughter to run to a neighbor's farm and telephone for help. He then grabbed the fire pump and walked into the smoke.

"It is warm behind the driftwood now, for the wind has gone with the geese. So would I—if I were the wind."

They found him early that afternoon, the victim of a heart attack, probably triggered by the heat and smoke. He had managed to set down the pump, stretch out on his back, fold his arms over his chest, and die as he had lived, with dignity, before a tendril of the fire passed lightly over him. His family was unhurt, save the terrible loss of husband and father. Also unhurt were the shack and the planted pines. That would have been important to him.

"The only conclusion I have ever reached is that I love all trees, but I am in love with pines."

When Leopold had purchased his original 80 acres along the Wisconsin River, in 1935, the land was an orphaned, denuded victim of ax and plow—a logged-over, worn-out cornfield—that would require painstaking work if it were ever to be natural again. The farmhouse had burned down, leaving only the chicken coop and a bleak row of elms to break the monotony—hardly the magical oak-savanna it had once been. Some Leopold scholars say he simply wanted the land to hunt and fish. Perhaps he did, in the beginning, but he was also a man of process, ever growing and learning. Not only would this land become a family retreat; it would also host an experiment still active half a century after his death: the restoration of a wild Wisconsin.

Today, the Aldo Leopold Memorial Reserve totals more than 1,400 acres of covenanted, privately owned floodplain forest, marshland, restored prairie, and oak-hickory-pine forest, administered by the Sand County Foundation and the Aldo Leopold Foundation. The shack, sometimes called "the most famous chicken coop in the world," still stands and is a National Historic Site, vastly unlike its 1935 condition.

Mother Estella had been daunted back then by the knee-deep manure piled along one wall. "When we carry it out and put it under your garden," her husband had said, "you'll be very glad it was there." He was right. In the years ahead nobody would enjoy the family retreat more than Estella. Her husband and children would treat her like a queen and do all the chores. They reinforced the walls with wooden planks washed up from the river. Then over the years they added a bunk wing, fireplace, chimney, and wooden floor and, together with friends, planted a staggering 36,000 pines.

The road to the shack is no longer straight. It curves gracefully and is

"There are some who can live without wild things, and some who cannot.... Like winds and sunsets, wild things were taken for granted until progress began to do away with them."

—ALDO LEOPOLD
*A SAND COUNTY ALMANAC*

flanked by tall trees as Leopold designed it, so each arc of the approach unveils new visual treasures. Rivers don't run straight; neither should roads.

Interstate 90/94, constructed in the early 1980s, is only a mile away, the faint drone of its traffic audible day and night. But more prominent are the 10,000-year-old post-glacial voices of Wisconsin, silenced when the land was cleared but now returned with the Leopold restoration: the chorus of jays, woodpeckers, finches, woodcocks, grouse, sparrows, and chickadees; the wind singing through oaks, maples, aspens, birches, and pines, all planted as acorns, seeds, and seedlings. Painstaking work, but also a labor of love.

"The landscape of any farm," Leopold wrote, "is the owner's portrait of himself." The old worn-out farm is now a mosaic of forest and prairie. The seedlings Leopold planted now tower 80 feet high as cathedral-like trees; and, as Leopold himself described it even in his lifetime, "the prairie flora…splashes its calendar of colors, from pink shooting-star in May to blue aster in October." There is no plaque or statue to Aldo Leopold— only the reserve itself, a living memorial.

He would have wanted it no other way.

"The wild things that live on my farm are reluctant to tell me, in so many words, how much of my township is included within their daily or nightly beat. I am curious about this, for it gives me the ratio between the size of their universe and the size of mine, and it conveniently begs the much more important question, who is the more thoroughly acquainted with the world in which he lives?"

Every available weekend the Leopold family would race out of Madison and up to the shack, back to the earth. Time to sleep on mattresses of canvas and hay. Time to cook and bake in the fireplace hearth, or, if outside, in the Dutch oven. Time to play guitars and sing into the night. Aldo would go to bed early and be up before the birds, listening, writing; his pencil, like his other tools—ax, shovel, eye, ear—always sharp. Metaphors of his mind. Dull tools made a dull man.

He would step outside into the sweetness of dawn.

"One hundred and twenty acres, according to the County Clerk, is the extent of my worldly domain. But the County Clerk is a sleepy fellow.…At daybreak I am the sole owner of all the acres I can walk over. It is not only the boundaries that disappear, but also the thought of being bounded."

He would sketch with words the parade of seasons:

*January:* "A rough-legged hawk comes sailing over the meadow ahead. Now he stops, hovers like a kingfisher, and then drops like a feathered bomb into the marsh."

*March:* "One swallow does not make a summer, but one skein of geese, cleaving the murk of a March thaw, is the spring.…It is an irony of history that the great powers should have discovered the unity of nations in Cairo in 1943. The geese of the world have had that notion for a longer time, and each March they stake their lives on its essential truth."

*May:* "When dandelions have set the mark of May on Wisconsin pastures, it is time to listen for the final proof of spring. Sit down on a tussock, cock your ears at the sky, dial out the bedlam of meadowlarks and redwings, and soon you may hear it: the flight-song of the upland plover, just now back from the Argentine."

*July:* "I can feel the sun now. The bird-chorus has run out of breath. The far clank of cowbells bespeaks a herd ambling to pasture. A tractor

> "When we see land as a community to which we belong, we may begin to use it with love and respect."
>
> —ALDO LEOPOLD
> *A SAND COUNTY ALMANAC*

roars warning that my neighbor is astir. The world has shrunk to those mean dimensions known to county clerks."

*September:* "It is on some, but not all, of these misty autumn daybreaks that one may hear the chorus of the quail. The silence is suddenly broken by a dozen contralto voices, no longer able to restrain their praise for the day to come. After a brief minute or two, the music closes as suddenly as it began."

*November:* "In the marsh, long windy waves surge across the grassy sloughs, beat against the far willows. A tree tries to argue, bare limbs waving, but there is no detaining the wind."

When Aldo Leopold was born in Burlington, Iowa, in 1887, his parents celebrated by planting a tree. He grew up with a father who taught him the outdoors and a mother who taught him classical literature. Armed with this Lincoln-like hybrid vigor, he enrolled in Yale Forest School in 1905, the same year that Gifford Pinchot, father of American forestry, convinced President Theodore Roosevelt to establish the U.S Forest Service. Pinchot was an imposing German-trained forester, who believed in the utilitarian dictum of conservation: Forests, he said, like all natural resources, should not be seen as inviolate sanctums as John Muir had espoused, but rather should be used wisely for the greatest good for the greatest number over the long run. Thus indoctrinated, young Leopold graduated in 1909 and traveled by train to Albuquerque and thence by stagecoach to the little town of Springerville, Arizona Territory, to begin duty as a Forest Service recruit in Apache National Forest, established only one year before. Never had he seen country so big and wild and wonderfully mysterious. "Like most people who see the landscapes of the Southwest for the first time," T. H. Watkins wrote of Leopold in *American Heritage* magazine, "he was immediately seduced by the clarity of light and the generosity of space."

Constellations of wildflowers brightened every meadow and oak grove. Cottonwood, willow, and sycamore flanked the canyon bottoms and trout-rich clear-water streams. A piñon and juniper forest enlivened the high desert. But Leopold was especially smitten by the handsome ponderosa pines commanding the Mogollon Rim, the great 300-mile-long igneous escarpment that runs from Flagstaff to New Mexico, right through the heart of Apache National Forest.

Higher still, aspen, spruce, and fir climbed into the mountains, including 11,590-foot Baldy Peak, the highest point in the forest, crowned by year-round snow and one of North America's southernmost alpine tundra plant communities. Black cinder cones broke the horizon. And the Blue Range, where Leopold would shoot the wolf and see the fierce green fire, had been described by an early forest inspector as "no well-defined mountain range, but rather a chaotic mass of very precipitous and rocky hills."

As wild as it seemed to young Leopold—not a single road dissected Apache National Forest then—this piece of Arizona was changing fast. Geronimo had been vanquished less than 30 years before, and now the wildlife was disappearing. Hunters had eliminated local bison and elk, and populations of antelope, mountain sheep, and mule deer were declining fast. Grizzlies, wolves, and mountain lions still haunted the hidden contours of canyon, rimrock, and mountain, imparting a wildness to the region, but

*FOLLOWING PAGES: Gray wolf, in black color phase, stands on the edge of sunlight and shadow in Montana. The ultimate hunter, it remains largely mythical and misunderstood, still persecuted by some, yet praised by others. A growing number of people see it as Leopold ultimately did: an indispensable element in the balance of nature.*

ALAN & SANDY CAREY

57

they also haunted the minds of local ranchers who called them varmints and vermin. Civilization was marching across America and would not be stopped. This was the heyday of predator control, when bounty hunters and government trappers arrived to kill varmints to make the land safe for people, cattle, and sheep. Leopold and his fellow foresters supported predator control as part of the Pinchot master plan to achieve wise and maximum use of a national forest. When copper mines opened in Clifton, to the south, the first demand for large volumes of timber fell onto Apache National Forest, and young Leopold helped organize the harvest.

But always hanging on the Apache horizon was the basaltic table-like mountain, Escudilla, an island of wild Arizona above the growing, deepening sea of tameness. Escudilla, like the dying wolf, would spark the beginning of Leopold's genesis from a Pinchot-minded, utilitarian forester to the enlightened founder of ecological conscience. On his first free Sunday morning, wearing cowboy hat and chaps, he rode his horse to the top of Escudilla, where he could feel the power of the mountain beneath him, for he knew, as everybody did, that somewhere in that rugged topography lived the legendary silver-tipped grizzly called Old Bigfoot.

"Old Bigfoot was a robber-baron," Leopold wrote years later "and Escudilla was his castle. Each spring, when the warm winds had softened the shadows on the snow, the old grizzly crawled out of his hibernation den in the rockslides and, descending the mountain, bashed in the head of a cow. Eating his fill, he climbed back to his crags, and there summered peaceably on marmots, conies, berries, and roots."

Nobody ever saw the bear, just its tracks, surely the largest in Arizona; and when anybody gazed pensively at Escudilla, always on the horizon, one thing came to mind: Old Bigfoot. Mountain and bear were the same, each a part of the other's mythology. Then progress arrived in the form of telephone wire, the automobile, and finally a government trapper, "a sort of St. George in overalls," Leopold remembered, "seeking dragons to slay at government expense. Were there, he asked, any destructive animals in need of slaying? Yes, there was the big bear." The trapper set out for Escudilla.

"In a month he was back," Leopold wrote, "his mule staggering under a heavy hide. There was only one barn in town big enough to dry it on. He had tried traps, poison, and all his usual wiles to no avail. Then he had erected a set-gun in a defile through which only the bear could pass, and waited. The last grizzly walked into the string and shot himself."

The skull went to the National Museum, where scientists quarreled over the bear's Latin name. No one argued on behalf of the bear, however, saying it had jurisdiction on Escudilla, and the right to kill one cow a year if it so desired. No one questioned the purpose or nobility of the clever trapper, or the need to make Arizona a better place to live. "It was only after we pondered on these things," Leopold wrote, "that we began to wonder who wrote the rules for progress."

Decades hence, he would grow to see the trapper and the bureau chief who sent him, and the congressmen who appropriated the funds, and even himself and the other foresters—all sons of pioneers—as instruments in the destruction of wildness. The congressmen, he wrote, "acclaimed the superior virtues of the frontiersman, but they strove with might and main to make an end of the frontier."

And of himself? "We forest officers, who acquiesced in the extin-

"The last word in ignorance is the man who says of an animal or plant: 'What good is it?' ...To keep every cog and wheel is the first precaution of intelligent tinkering."

—ALDO LEOPOLD
*ROUND RIVER*

guishment of the bear, knew a local rancher who had plowed up a dagger engraved with the name of one of Coronado's captains. We spoke harshly of the Spaniards who, in their zeal for gold and converts, had needlessly extinguished the native Indians. It did not occur to us that we, too, were the captains of an invasion too sure of its own righteousness.

"Escudilla still hangs on the horizon, but when you see it you no longer think of bear. It's only a mountain now."

After two years in Arizona, where Leopold distinguished himself as a bright, respected, and hardworking forester, he was transferred to the troubled Carson National Forest of northern New Mexico and promoted to deputy supervisor. Soon thereafter, in 1912, he married Estella Bergere, considered the most loved and respected girl in New Mexico, and was promoted again, this time to supervisor. At 26 he had a new wife and his own national forest.

Overgrazing by sheep had deeply impoverished portions of the Carson, leaving valleys once verdant with grasses naked and gullied with erosion. Some soils had washed away; others were impacted to where trees could not regenerate. The land was dying, and Leopold knew it. The Forest Service's policy of individual grazing allotments had been supported by the U.S. Supreme Court only the year before in California and Colorado, and now Leopold moved to initiate it in Carson National Forest. His determination infected those around him. "By God," he said, "the Individual Allotment and every other reform we have promised is going to *stick*—even if it takes a six-shooter to do it."

It might have been bravado, but it worked. Leopold won the respect of foresters and sheepmen alike, and the land began to heal.

The following spring a late storm of sleet, rain, and hail caught him on horseback near the Continental Divide, and by the time he arrived back in Santa Fe he was nearly dead with acute nephritis. During some 16 months of recovery he edited the *Pine Cone,* a Carson National Forest newsletter, and read voraciously: Thoreau's journals (a wedding gift from his mother), old issues of NATIONAL GEOGRAPHIC and *Atlantic Monthly,* and of special significance William Temple Hornaday's *Our Vanishing Wild Life* (purchased for his father). Hornaday's words were a clarion call that cemented a conviction then developing in Leopold's mind: that America needed to take quick and drastic measures to safeguard her magnificent but threatened game species. "The book galvanized Aldo's conviction," wrote Curt Meine, a Leopold biographer. "The facts and fears had been long known, but Hornaday's uncompromising polemics gave new urgency to the issue. The message sank in as Aldo's long months of recuperation continued. His focus began to shift, slowly, certainly, and irreversibly."

He returned to work with slowly growing vigor, broadening his expertise as a self-taught wildlife ecologist, soil scientist, and range manager. He authored a handbook on game and fish management and worked tirelessly to convince local hunters to form affiliates of the American Game Protective Association. In an issue of the revived *Pine Cone* Leopold wrote, "As the cone scatters the seeds of the pine and fir tree, so may it scatter the seeds of wisdom and understanding among men, to the end that every citizen may learn to hold the lives of harmless wild creatures as a public trust for human good, against the abuse of which he stands personally responsible. Thus, and only thus, will our wild life be preserved."

His words won praise from no less an admirer than former President Theodore Roosevelt, himself an outdoorsman, who in 1917 wrote, "I think your platform simply capital."

For many that would have been an end in itself; for Leopold it was just the beginning. By 1921 he had chewed on Pinchot's dicta of development and utilitarianism long enough to "raise the question of whether the policy of development…should continue to govern in absolutely every instance, or whether the principle of highest use does not itself demand that representative portions of some forests be preserved as wilderness."

Leopold was beginning to understand what John Muir had always known: that only by saving wild America will America save itself from the artificial machinelike metronome of a fully automated, mechanized world. What Muir had written with poetry and passion Leopold would augment with academic brilliance and practical economics.

In late May 1924 he packed up his young family and departed Albuquerque for Madison, Wisconsin, to be assistant director of the Forest Products Laboratory. Five days after he left, his recreational working plan was quietly initiated by the Forest Service in New Mexico, creating the Gila Wilderness Area, the first such officially designated area in America.

Wisconsin was home now, but Leopold, disenchanted with the "industrial motif" of his job, left the Forest Service in 1928 to conduct a privately-funded nationwide survey of habitat conditions and game populations, the most thorough of its kind ever undertaken. From the experience came two groundbreaking publications, in the second of which, a 1933 textbook entitled *Game Management,* he concluded: "In short, twenty centuries of 'progress' have brought the average citizen a vote, a national anthem, a Ford, a bank account, and a high opinion of himself, but not the capacity to live in high density without befouling and denuding his environment, nor a conviction that such capacity, rather than such density, is the true test of whether he is civilized. The practice of game management may be one of the means of developing a culture which will meet this test."

The University of Wisconsin offered Leopold a professorship in game management, the first of its kind in the country. He accepted and held the position the rest of his life. "The professor," his students and acquaintances called him. A pipe in one hand, a pencil in the other, balding and bespectacled, he was a lean fence post of a man with a restless intellect, often thinking serious things. Aloof at times, but always a gentleman. On a final exam he asked: "Select one plant or animal which you saw on the campus today and discuss its role in Wisconsin history." He taught his children as well. His eldest son, Starker, recalled: "Dad would pick one of us out and ask, 'What did you learn today?' Not what had you *done* that day but what you had *learned*—a big difference."

The same year he bought his farm, 1935, he traveled to Germany to study the meticulously managed forests there. What he saw were not forests at all, but artificial rows of trees absent of a rich and varied understory. "I never realized before," he wrote, "that the melodies of nature are music only when played against the undertones of evolutionary history. In the German forest…one now hears only a dismal fugue out of the timeless reaches of the carboniferous." Dismayed at the idea that America's forests, if logged again and again, could someday become as sterile, Leopold joined a handful of devoted preservationists, rallied by the young forester, Robert Marshall, to create the Wilderness Society. "This country has been swinging the hammer of development so long and so hard," Leopold wrote, "that it has forgotten the anvil of wilderness which gave value and significance to its labors."

On his farm he planted buckwheat and partridge pea to attract quail; Sudan grass, sorghum, and millet for wintering bobwhites and pheasants; grapevine for cover. And of course trees, always more trees; he planted them even after drought had killed 90 percent of a previous year's efforts. Back in Madison, he nourished his students and worked tirelessly on academic and conservation committees, all the while sharpening his land ethic: "There is as yet no ethic dealing with man's relation to land and to the animals and plants which grow upon it.... The land-relation is still strictly economic, entailing privileges but not obligations.... Obligations have no meaning without conscience, and the problem we face is the extension of the social conscience from people to land."

With the publication of *A Sand County Almanac* in 1949, the year after he died, Aldo Leopold became the ecology movement's impresario.

His children scattered with the wind to pursue distinguished careers in science and conservation. In 1976 his daughter Nina moved back to the Leopold Reserve. She and her husband, Charlie, cut down some pines—in need of thinning—and built a log home and research center within a mile and a half of the shack.

Still active and alert in their 70s, Nina and Charlie keep a list of local flowering, breeding, and migration times posted on their wall.

*January 7:* Wisconsin River freezes over. *February 28:* Canada geese arrive. *March 13:* Red-winged blackbirds on cattails. *April 3:* First song of the wood frog. *May 1:* Rose-breasted grosbeak arrives. *June 26:* White prairie clover blooms. *July 12:* Cardinal sings its second song. *August 23:* Turtlehead blooms. *September 17:* Red maple turns color. *October 16:* Last swim in the pond (for Nina and Charlie). *November 11:* First accumulation of snow. *December 2:* Pond freezes (in center).

"That land is a community is the basic concept of ecology," Leopold wrote, "but that land is to be loved and respected is an extension of ethics."

And family.

Generations come and go and leave their signatures on the land, some less indelibly than before. They've read *A Sand County Almanac* and confirmed that one person can make a difference. Leopold's genius was his vision and his voice—more a gentle plea than a pontification—to help us see land and all the wild things on it as an opportunity to exercise responsibilities as much as rights. Minds dedicated to strict and narrow economics might secure one form of wealth, he said, but sacrifice another.

At what point in our pursuit of progress and addiction to growth do we lose more than we gain?

"We shall never achieve harmony with land," he wrote, "any more than we shall achieve justice or liberty for people. In these higher aspirations the important thing is not to achieve, but to strive...."

And so he did.

Up before dawn, with binoculars and a bird whistle around his neck, he walked his Wisconsin land and planted trees, thinking like a mountain.

> "The basic question is whether a hawkless, owl-less countryside is a livable countryside for Americans with eyes to see and ears to hear."
>
> —ALDO LEOPOLD
> *ROUND RIVER*

"On motionless wing they emerge...and settle in clangorous descending spirals to their feeding grounds....The ultimate value in these marshes is wildness, and the crane is wildness incarnate."

—ALDO LEOPOLD, *A SAND COUNTY ALMANAC*

*Having migrated south for the winter, sandhill cranes gather in the sienna waters of Florida's Myakka River State Park (left), and New Mexico's Bosque del Apache National Wildlife Refuge (above). Come spring, they will fly in great numbers, and at great heights, to their northern breeding grounds.*

*PRECEDING PAGES: Clear and tranquil, the West Fork of the Gila River glides through the Gila Wilderness—the first officially designated wilderness area in the United States—in New Mexico's Gila National Forest.*

# "I have seen many birds of beauty, but not one of such dazzling plumage...."

—ALDO LEOPOLD
*LETTER, MAY 1904*

*Admired by Leopold for its blue plumage, the indigo bunting (right), traditionally breeding in the eastern U.S., is expanding its range into the West and Southwest. In Wisconsin's Aldo Leopold Memorial Reserve marsh grasses (below) burgeon, along with pine forests and other natural habitats. The Leopold shack (opposite), "the most famous chicken coop in the world," stands amid trees planted by family and friends.*

*FOLLOWING PAGES: A ruffed grouse flies in alarm from evergreen boughs. Of ruffed grouse, Leopold wrote: "Summer windfalls keep their dried leaves, and during snows each windfall harbors a grouse."*

BATES LITTLEHALES

LAYNE KENNEDY; KIM HEACOX (RIGHT); S. NIELSEN/DRK PHOTO (FOLLOWING PAGES)

"If...we can live without goose music, we may as well do away with stars, or sunsets...."

—ALDO LEOPOLD, *ROUND RIVER*

"*O*ne swallow does not make a summer," Leopold observed, "but one skein of geese, cleaving the murk of a March thaw, is the spring." Sunrise on the Wisconsin River (below), seen from the Aldo Leopold Memorial Reserve, offers a glimpse of the morning magic that attracted the family here to cultivate things wild and free.

FOLLOWING PAGES: A living paean, these white pines—Leopold's most beloved tree—stand where he planted them, on the Aldo Leopold Memorial Reserve, formerly overgrazed and eroded savanna, woods, wetlands, and devitalized farmer's fields.

# BURN CANDLES
# WITH
# INDEPENDENCE

# Bob Marshall and the Freedom of the Wilderness

BOB MARSHALL

On New Year's Eve, 1930, Pioneer Hall in the little town of Wiseman, Alaska, pulsed with music and dancing. Most of the men were gold miners who'd traveled from the frozen reaches of the upper Koyukuk River and now sported the only clean shirts they owned or could borrow. Many of the women were Eskimos who wore their finest print dresses and beaded moccasins. Children scampered about the dance hall playing games, while babies slept on benches in the anteroom. Outside, the winter air was cold enough to make your teeth ache; firewood burst apart with the strike of an ax. The indigo night had settled down like iron, as Wiseman, one degree north of the Arctic Circle, was sunless from early December to early January. Inside the hall, however, the warm festivities might last for 11 hours—8 p.m. until 7 a.m.—as everybody enjoyed celebrating and catching up on news.

Somebody announced a square dance, and Bob Marshall jumped to his feet. A bundle of exuberance two days shy of his 30th birthday, he'd come to Wiseman not in search of gold but of adventure and blank places on the map. He made a distinctive first impression with his toothy smile, round face, and protruding ears. Within the man lived a quick wit, fierce intelligence, and an undying passion to keep wilderness wild. "If I had only been born in time to join the Lewis and Clark expedition," he'd lamented in his youth. At age 11, while sick with pneumonia in New York City, he'd read a book about Lewis and Clark that made such an impression on him he reread it every year for the next decade.

The world wasn't as wild as it used to be, but Marshall would still find a vast frontier in Arctic Alaska. For him the art of exploration would be just that: an art—something deeper and more responsible than the invasive self-servings of earlier explorers. "As I see it," he observed, "Peary's discovery of the North Pole, Amundsen's journey to the South Pole, Byrd's junketing in Antarctica, or the impending ascent of Mount Everest do not make the road of humanity as a whole the least bit happier."

Marshall would find happiness in the humble, self-reliant people with

*Grizzly bear, symbol of Alaskan wildness, surveys its domain of roadless, Arctic tundra.*

*PRECEDING PAGES: Lenticular clouds indicate high winds, blowing storms into Montana's northern Rockies where Bob Marshall hiked the high country.*

him that New Year's Eve, people surrounded by a landscape that inspired and challenged them. "Most important of all," he would write, "happiness in the Koyukuk is stimulated by the prevalent philosophy of enjoying life as it passes along. The absence of constant worry about the future and remorse about the past destroys much that tends to make men miserable."

The music accelerated, and Marshall hit the dance floor. "Bob loved to square-dance," a friend once recalled. "I don't know why, he just loved it. He was a real funny square dancer. He just *bounced* around, which was part of his personality."

Earlier that year, in 1930, he'd earned a Ph.D. in plant physiology from Johns Hopkins University, adding to his previous degrees from Harvard and the New York State College of Forestry. He flaunted none of them; titles meant little to him. And though he'd come north ostensibly to study tree growth at the northern timberline, his greatest fascination would be with the people themselves, "the independent, exciting, and friendly life of the Arctic frontier....the civilization of whites and Eskimos which flourishes in the upper reaches of the Koyukuk, 200 miles beyond the edge of the Twentieth Century."

After an evening of dancing or conversation in Wiseman, he would "walk home through the freezing air, while the northern lights rolled brightly across the heavens, and feel that life could not be more splendid."

In his one-room, 16-by-18-foot log cabin, he would play classics on his phonograph—the *Hungarian Rhapsody,* the *Gymnopedie,* Ravel's *Bolero,* Schubert's *Unfinished Symphony*—to end yet another great day. "The last record for the evening I always put on just before turning out the gasoline lantern," he recalled, "and then I listened to it comfortably from bed. When the final note was over and the automatic stop had clicked, it generally took me about thirty seconds to fall asleep."

Despite his Eastern pedigree, Marshall was easily at home in this rugged, frigid, northwestern world. His friends were his riches, and he made them easily. "Any attempt to understand Bob Marshall," wrote a biographer, James M. Glover, "must begin with his father. For it was through him that Bob acquired much of his humor, his humanitarianism, and especially his environmental activism. Louis Marshall was a brilliant constitutional lawyer, a prominent Jewish leader, and an eloquent champion of minority rights. He was also an ardent naturalist and a staunch defender of wilderness in the Adirondacks." Affectionately called "Pop" by his children, he never owned a car and seldom went to movies. In the last nine years of his life, while Bob lived away from home, Louis wrote him more than 500 letters. When he died in 1929, Bob lamented, "There was in the woods a tremendous natural tie between us, a bond which is indeed painful to realize is broken forever."

What childhood could be misspent in the Adirondack Mountains of upstate New York? Here the Marshall family owned a summer cabin at Knoll-wood—a thickly forested hillside overlooking Lower Saranac Lake—where young Bob, together with his two brothers and one sister, learned the joys and freedoms of long days in the outdoors. Traveling by train and boat, Bob first came to Knollwood from New York City in the summer of 1901 when he was six months old. Here amid sentinel-like hemlocks, birches, and spruces; games of baseball and tennis; and evenings on the cabin porch while Pop read aloud with great drama from James Fenimore Cooper and Charles Dickens, Bob savored all or part of his first 25 summers.

"We admired the fine trees, beautiful flowers, lights and shades among the trees," he wrote at 15, "and the hundreds of other things which make the woods so superior to the city."

The cabin sat back from the lake, hidden by woods that Pop refused to cut down to improve the view. When timber thieves continued to harvest state-owned trees in the Adirondacks, Pop berated them for being "as great an enemy of the public as one guilty of treason." And of the trains that sparked fires in the dry season, he asked the forest, fish, and game commissioner, "What has the State done? It has lain by supinely and permitted the railroads which run through the forests to employ locomotives which are so many instruments of arson."

Bob Marshall witnessed it all and came to believe, as his father did, that no adversary was too great or mountain too high. His time at Knollwood instilled in him joy, passion, heart, and mind, not unlike young King Arthur's apprenticeship to the wisdom of Merlin. Wilderness would be Marshall's Excalibur, his sword in the stone.

"I was privileged," he later recalled of his childhood, "to explore the mighty tract bounded by the Forest Home Road, the Knollwood Road, Lower Saranac Lake, and Fish Creek—an immense expanse, about three-quarters of a mile by three-eighths of a mile, in which one could, with diligence, occasionally get beyond the sounds of civilization. This almost trailless area was a real wilderness to me, as exciting in a different way as the unexplored continent which I had missed by my tardy birth."

In the summer of 1918 he climbed Whiteface Mountain, his first significant summit, once described as "the most graceful of all Adirondack peaks." His brother George accompanied him, as did Herb Clark, the amiable guide who was their teacher and friend. Then came Mounts Marcy and Algonquin, the two highest Adirondack summits, and soon thereafter Mount Iroquois, the seventh highest. The views intoxicated the men; there would be no turning back. Bob and George hiked like the wind— Bob sometimes 40 miles a day—and in 1925 they became the first to scale all 46 of the 4,000-foot peaks in the Adirondacks.

If Marshall was racing time to find his own terra incognita before the world did, he would need to turn west. From 1925 to 1928 he explored the Bitterroot Country of Idaho and Montana while employed at the Northern Rocky Mountain Forest Experiment Station in Missoula. He quickly impressed his fellow foresters with his sense of humor and his prowess as a hiker. On days when work was slow, fire lookouts would call into their district offices to place wagers on the exact time Marshall would finish another 40-mile hike. Even when the train that had carried him to Missoula in June 1925 had broken down just outside Iowa, he had immediately gotten off and hiked 30 miles in ten hours—returning in time to board the repaired train and continue westward.

Montana was fertile ground for the budding preservationist, but Alaska would be his greatest adventure, where he could set his watch back a hundred years. He first arrived in Wiseman in the summer of 1929, landing at the airstrip on July 22 in a one-engine, seven-passenger Hamilton cabin plane, which the pilot had operated, he remembered, "with great skill and without a good map." They were warmly greeted by smiling strangers and given

"[A] ...singular aspect of the wilderness is that it gratifies every one of the senses."

—ROBERT MARSHALL
*ALASKA WILDERNESS*

a dance in their honor at Pioneer Hall. Marshall learned that as many as a hundred people inhabited Wiseman and the surrounding drainage of the Middle Fork of the Koyukuk River but that the neighboring North Fork was peopleless and largely unexplored.

Three days later he and his partner, Al Retzlaf, loaded up their horses, Brownie and Bronco, and followed the dirt road northwest out of Wiseman. They crossed into the North Fork drainage and headed toward the crest of the Brooks Range. On the seventh day they ascended a ridge and gazed at a wondrous scene. "The view from the top gave us an excellent idea of the jagged country toward which we were heading," Marshall wrote. "The main Brooks Range divide was entirely covered with snow. Close at hand, only about ten miles air line to the north, was a precipitous pair of mountains, one on each side of the North Fork. I bestowed the name of Gates of the Arctic on them, christening the east portal Boreal Mountain and the west portal Frigid Crags."

Perhaps Marshall realized that in finding this nameless region, and in naming it, he and Retzlaf had become their own Lewis and Clark. The lessons of history were not beyond him; the last thing he wanted was to initiate the same pioneer spirit that had fenced, paved, and tamed much of the contiguous United States. "Because the unique recreational value of Alaska lies in its frontier character," he wrote, "it would seem desirable to establish a really sizeable area, free from roads and industries, where frontier conditions will be preserved....In the name of a balanced use of American resources, let's keep northern Alaska largely a wilderness!"

Half a century later, in December 1980 under President Jimmy Carter, the Alaska National Interest Lands Conservation Act (ANILCA) became law, creating seven new national parks that more than doubled the acreage in the U.S. National Park Service system. A diamond among the jewels would be the 8.5-million-acre Gates of the Arctic National Park and Preserve, the second largest National Park Service unit in the United States, nearly four times larger than Yellowstone.

It would become a fitting tribute to Marshall's wilderness élan, but one he would never live to see. For now, he and Retzlaf could think only of the terrain ahead, the thrill of the unknown, the aggravation of mosquitoes and tussocks, the "austere grandeur" of the Valley of Precipices and the horses bolting away with the approach of Griz, the dreaded bear. "I managed to halt Brownie at the tent long enough to snatch up the gun which lay near the door," Marshall wrote, "but he continued dragging me down the valley toward Bronco, who had paused in crazed disturbance, waiting for his comrade. Meanwhile the bear kept approaching the tent, the horses kept growing more agitated, and I was being dragged farther from home and possessions. I could not take aim at the bear without dropping the halter and losing Brownie, so I shot from my waist without aiming, still holding the halter rope tightly. I thought I would scare the bear, but the shot must have echoed, because the grizzly seemed to imagine it came from behind him. Anyway, he proceeded with doubled speed toward the tent. Now I knew there was no choice but to let Brownie go and shoot in earnest. I hit the bear, but not fatally and he turned around and retreated into the hills."

Upriver, Marshall discovered "a towering, black, unscalable-looking giant, the highest peak in this section of the Brooks Range." He called it

"There is something glorious in traveling beyond the ends of the earth..., in cutting loose from the bonds of world-wide civilization."

—ROBERT MARSHALL
*ALASKA WILDERNESS*

"Matterhorn of the Koyukuk, although it looked less ascendable than its celebrated Swiss namesake." He would later name it Mount Doonerak, from an Eskimo term meaning, according to Marshall, a spirit "delighting in making trouble."

By the time he and Retzlaf returned to Wiseman 23 days after departing, Marshall was in love with Arctic Alaska and its gracious people. It was the cold that made them warm, the distances that made them close, the independence that made them dependable. Never had he encountered such a free and honest society or witnessed such daily self-reliance. It confirmed what he already suspected: that the best lives prosper in close communion with nature. He flew home to New York, but by August 1930 he returned to Wiseman, this time to rent a cabin and stay for nearly 13 months, until September 1931.

America was crippled by the Great Depression, yet Wiseman maintained a dignity free of bankruptcy, breadlines, and soup kitchens. People came here to live more than to make a living, to measure success through the simplest of moral prisms. Poverty was not poverty, or wealth wealth, as everybody chopped wood and hauled water and found their riches in truth, honesty, friendship, and family. To see the northern lights, to mush sled dogs through winter's white silence, to hike through summer's bright wildflowers, to grow a garden and catch a grayling—that was true wealth.

"I've had plenty of opportunities to go Outside but I never wanted to go," one longtimer told Marshall. "Every one is elbowing one another and putting on fancy airs, and a poor man can't hardly make enough to eat. Here you always have plenty to live on at worst, lots of caribou and small game to eat, and you can grow all the potatoes and garden truck you want. There's no rent to pay, an easy chance to get at least a share in a good [mining] claim, and nobody in God's world to boss your life except yourself."

"Outside it's a rush and a push and a jam all the time," said another, "and if you drop something somebody else is going to pick it up. Here you've got time to read and to think and to enjoy yourself. And anyway, I like these hills, and I've lived around here thirty-three years, and no place else could ever seem like home."

Marshall explored the Arctic by snowshoe, boat, and dogsled and began writing a book, published in 1933, that would become a best-seller: *Arctic Village*.

Since his boyhood days on the baseball field at Knollwood, he had compiled statistics on nearly everything quantifiable. This extended into his work out West, where he recorded the eating habits and profanity quotients of loggers and the pancake consumption of Forest Service employees.

Now in Wiseman, he noted the residents' ages and their financial summaries, job skills, dancing times, reading materials, and even the number of minutes they spent discussing various topics: from gossip (highest) to work (second highest) to Alaskan politics and local history (both relatively low) to plans for more than three months ahead (lowest).

On the subject of labor Marshall wrote: "It is interesting to observe the enthusiasm which is taken in doing a job well merely for the satisfaction which a neat piece of workmanship brings."

On transportation: "Yet withal, there is nothing in the Arctic as valuable, and in many ways as admirable, as a good dog. The amount of freight these animals have hauled is staggering. I know of a team of four strong

*FOLLOWING PAGES: To see Alaska's aurora borealis, or northern lights, rolling "brightly across the heavens," wrote Marshall, reminded him that despite the cold, dark isolation of winter, "life could not be more splendid."*

malemutes (the type of dog used in the Koyukuk) which hauled a load of 1,100 pounds a distance of sixty-four miles in three days."

And on food, garnished with humor, he observed: "I only recall three expositions on cooking technique during all my stay in the Koyukuk. One was for blueberry cold jam, one was for that sheep meat *Bordelaise,* and one was for cooking a porcupine. The last went as follows: 'Place the porcupine and a rock in some boiling water. Cook until you can shove a fork into the rock. Then throw out the porcupine and eat the rock.'"

One of Marshall's best insights into Eskimo culture came with the aid of music. Of his many friends who regularly dropped by his cabin, one was a Kobuk Eskimo named Nutirwik. Marshall wrote of him in *Alaska Wilderness:* "This small man—he was scarcely more than five feet tall—with his thin face, high cheekbones, and little gnarled hands more than held his own with his sturdier-looking companions. His prominent eyebrows were in sharp contrast with his thin eyes. He had a strong, sensitive face and remarkably few wrinkles for a man close to sixty who had lived out of doors all his life. His name literally means blizzard. When he came to live among the whites about 1903 he changed it to Harry Snowden, but we continued to use his Eskimo name…."

Marshall played some records on his phonograph for him. Harry listened politely but without enthusiasm. Then Marshall played Ravel's *Bolero.* "He had previously sat through half a dozen popular songs with the most complete lack of expression on his face that I can imagine in a human being…," Marshall remembered. "Then timorously I tried the *Bolero,* and almost at the first notes Harry was completely transformed….At the end he was in ecstasy and exclaimed: 'Gee, isn't there a lot of playing, isn't there a lot of music going on there! Play it again, Bob!'"

This perplexed Marshall until a few weeks later when he stopped near the abandoned village of Coldfoot, south of Wiseman. It was a chilled October night, with snow on the mountains and a cold darkness descending from the north. The wind and freezing waters of a nearby creek seemed to him a symphony, "sometimes rising to a great crescendo, sometimes dying down so that I could hear nothing but the unending, but constantly varying, rushing of the water. It reminded me of the drum undertone which runs through the entire *Bolero,* never the same at any two instants, but still exactly the same throughout the whole composition. All at once it occurred to me why the Eskimos were so enthusiastic about the *Bolero.* Because the *Bolero* is a perfect counterpart of the music they have heard from earliest childhood out in the wilderness of the North. The drums are the rivers rumbling unvaryingly, and the rest of the orchestra is the wind howling, the ice cracking, snowslides coming down the mountains, rocks tumbling over one another, the wild animals howling. It represents to the natives all the chaotic music of nature in its wildest moments."

Back home in the East, Marshall received a steady stream of letters from friends in Alaska, some running to 30 pages. *Arctic Village* was favorably received, even winning praise from the critic's critic, H. L. Mencken, who wrote of the Wisemanites: "They have no politicians. Their police force is rudimentary and impotent. Above all, they are not cursed with theologians….They are freer to be intelligent, and what is more, decent."

Marshall dedicated the book "to the people of the Koyukuk who have made for themselves the happiest civilization…." He shared royalties among

"No comfort, no security, no invention... which the modern world had to offer could provide half the elation of the days spent in the...Arctic wilderness."

—ROBERT MARSHALL
*ALASKA WILDERNESS*

them, saving a little for "those children who will come of age in the future."

The idyllic Arctic life portrayed by Marshall was not without its problems. He noted that the suicide rate there was some seven times higher than in the rest of the United States and that alcohol was already a scourge among the Eskimos. Yet overall the Koyukuk remained a crucible of freedom where the laws of nature were the laws of men, where people could spread their wings and discover their abilities and determine their fates. It would remain this way, Marshall believed, only as long as the country was wild and undeveloped. Wilderness was a blueprint for freedom.

He concluded, "The inhabitants of the Koyukuk would rather eat beans with liberty, burn candles with independence, and mush dogs with adventure than have the luxury and the restrictions of the outside world. A person misses many things by living in the isolation of the Koyukuk, but he gains a life filled with an amount of freedom, tolerance, beauty, and contentment such as few human beings are ever fortunate enough to achieve."

Marshall returned to the East as exuberant as always, still a forester, and more focused than ever on preserving wilderness. Alarmed by the rate of deforestation across the country and the blindness of professional foresters to it, he analyzed hundreds of articles in *American Forests,* the magazine of the American Forestry Association (AFA), and found most of them extraneous if not shallow. Only eight percent discussed "forest conservation problems." He wrote to the president of the AFA, who defended his organization. But Marshall also sent a copy to Gifford Pinchot, the nation's forester emeritus and now governor of Pennsylvania, who agreed with him a hundred percent.

The summer of 1932 found Marshall enjoying precious days in the Adirondacks. On July 15 he hiked 19 hours (3:30 a.m. until 10:30 p.m.) and bagged 14 summits—a single-day record—ascending a total of 13,600 feet. That same month he climbed Maine's Mount Katahdin and later told Percival Baxter, Maine's governor, that he "remember[ed] vividly the grand spectacle looking northwest from its summit toward [what was then] the largest forest area in the United States without any roads in it."

Hiking and climbing filled him with euphoria but conservation battles beckoned, and that September he moved to Washington, D.C., to work again for the U.S. Forest Service, this time on a Senate-authorized report on the overall status of U.S. forests. He compiled a list of roadless areas and recommended that no less than 55 million acres be designated as "primitive," and thus off-limits to development. The request was passed along to regional foresters who, according to biographer James Glover, "responded with the enthusiasm of the stone faces on Easter Island." There were timber interests to think of, they said, and mining and grazing. Multiple-use utilitarianism was the doctrine of the day. Marshall wondered if these men considered forestry less a science than a trade school. He badgered them— he was his father's son—and wrote to one in Missoula: "I do wish that you would hurry up and get that entire country…set aside as wilderness before some damn fool chamber of commerce or some nonsensical organizer of unemployed demands a useless highway to provide work and a market for hotdogs and gasoline."

"How much wilderness do we really need?" a skeptic asked him. Marshall replied: "How many Brahms symphonies do we need?"

Yet the forests continued to fall as saws echoed through the Pacific Northwest, Montana, California, Colorado, the Appalachians, even Marshall's beloved Adirondacks. By 1930, 42,000 miles of roads sliced through the national forests, and thousands more were planned. Science alone could not save wild America. Neither could government. What was needed, Marshall believed, was "an organization of spirited people who will fight for the freedom of the wilderness." We need room for adventure, he said: places to get lost and found, to face peril, to test our physical limits, to sharpen our wits. Places to learn humility and practice grace. "Life without the chance for such exertions," he concluded, "would be for many persons a dreary game, scarcely bearable in its horrible banality."

So it was in January 1935 that Marshall and a handful of other men met at the Cosmos Club in Washington, D.C., to found the Wilderness Society. "We want no straddlers," Marshall announced; it was time to "battle uncompromisingly" to protect what few roadless areas remained in America.

By now his public life had melded with his private one. He squeezed every hour out of every day, traveling widely as director of forestry and grazing within the U.S. Office of Indian Affairs. Yet he found time to date several women, all of whom enjoyed the outdoors. "Gee whiz, this is great," he'd exclaim as he breezed up mountain trails or ran through his brother's home with his nephew on his shoulders. He remained the chief financier and unabashed champion of the Wilderness Society, often urging satellite organizations such as the Quetico-Superior Committee and the Adirondack Mountain Club to stand firm in the paths of highway engineers.

In August 1936 Marshall hurried home to Saranac Lake, where his sister Putey was gravely ill with cancer. What he found, he said, "wasn't Putey, but really some stranger dying under whatever comfort drugs could give." Her death at age 38 deeply saddened him. He remembered their youth when "we rowed among the Islands and explored the deep bays of Saranac Lake while the sky changed from blue to red to black sparkling with stars, and the pine trees faded from detailed, three dimensional living objects to black silhouettes against the red sunset. Those days with Putey were so glorious, so peaceful, that I used to think up some sort of life which would keep me permanently at Knollwood and frequently with her."

He returned to the Forest Service the following year as chief of recreation and lands, an important job he tackled with gusto. But the North was calling, and in August 1938 he returned to Wiseman to see old friends and to climb Mount Doonerak. It was a glorious reunion as he danced at the roadhouse and played ball with the Eskimo children. Then he and three companions whom he judged "outstandingly competent wilderness travelers" floated down the Middle Fork of the Koyukuk in an old wooden tub they called "the raft." They turned upriver at the North Fork and for six days—11 hours a day—battled the current as they pushed, pulled, poled, and carried the raft to a base camp below Doonerak.

The weather was horrible. The rain pounded them, then turned to snow. They headed back downriver and nearly died when their raft spilled them into the frigid water, the current sweeping them into a tunnel through a gravel bank. Gasping for breath and numb with cold, they pulled themselves ashore and with shaking hands built fires to dry out. Twenty-nine days after departing, the bedraggled foursome returned to Wiseman. Such a trip would have dispirited if not killed most men, but Marshall measured it with good cheer: "For a purely good time without any anti-social by-products it would be hard to beat four weeks' adventure in unexplored wilderness."

Was Bob Marshall packing an entire lifetime into a few years? Did he know his time was short? "The variable which to me seems to make the difference between a tragic and a normal death," he wrote, "is the factor of happiness; a dual factor embracing both the personal happiness of the one who died and the amount he did toward making other people happy."

His schedule was typically busy the night of November 10, 1939, when he boarded the midnight train from Washington, D.C., to New York City. He appeared in good health. But when the train pulled into Pennsylvania Station, he was found dead in his berth, only 38, the same age as Putey when she died.

His vast circle of family and friends was devastated. Two months earlier he had fallen ill in Washington State and had been told by a doctor to go home and rest. He blithely said it was sunstroke and indigestion, nothing to worry about. Others later speculated he had a heart problem and knew something was seriously wrong. His long hours and hikes did not abate. There was so much to do, so much to see, so much to save of this wild and wondrous world. Then, like the brightest comet in the sky, he was gone.

In August 1940 a 950,000-acre roadless area in the Flathead and Lewis and Clark National Forests of Montana was designated the Bob Marshall Wilderness Area, known by millions today as "the Bob." A mountain in the Adirondacks also bears his name. And Adirondack Park has grown to some six million acres, nearly half of which is forest preserve to remain forever wild. The town of Saranac Lake bustles in busy seasons, but the lake itself, like Knollwood, remains relatively peaceful and still.

The entire sweep of Arctic Alaska did not escape industrialization as Bob had wished. The Dalton Highway and the trans-Alaska oil pipeline, built to Prudhoe Bay in the 1970s, run along the Middle Fork of the Koyukuk right past Wiseman. Large 18-wheel trucks shatter the silence, and summer tour buses pull into town to see log cabins, sled dogs, and satellite dishes. The roadhouse has fallen down, and Marshall's cabin is gone. But in its place a thicket of birch and spruce reaches for the sky.

He would smile at that—the forester's cabin reclaimed by a forest.

West of Wiseman, Arctic Alaska stretches into Gates of the Arctic National Park and Preserve, Kobuk Valley National Park, and Noatak National Preserve; to the east lies the Arctic National Wildlife Refuge—a total of some 36 million acres of protected lands, much of it designated wilderness.

A fine legacy. Another smile.

"The average person, living in mechanized civilization," he concluded in *Arctic Village,* "has small opportunity for genuine adventure. But there is not a person past infancy in the entire Koyukuk who cannot look back on repeated adventures which would put to shame the imaginative tales consumed by millions of thrill-starved citizens of the United States. There is an exultation in snowshoeing at mid-winter to the Arctic Divide, in meeting the hazards involved in the passage of some swollen wilderness river, in subsisting a hundred miles from the closest human being, which adds tone, vitality, and color to the entire functioning of life."

It's not when you die that mattered to Bob Marshall; it's how you live.

> "And now I found myself here …with dozens of never-visited valleys and hundreds of unscaled summits still as virgin as during their Paleozoic creation."
>
> —ROBERT MARSHALL
> *ALASKA WILDERNESS*

# "...discovering an unpeopled universe where only the laws of nature held sway."

—ROBERT MARSHALL
*ALASKA WILDERNESS*

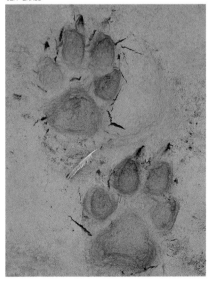

*The North Fork of the Koyukuk River (opposite), one of six officially designated "wild and scenic rivers" in Gates of the Arctic National Park, runs below the red bearberry slopes of Boreal Mountain. Signs of hunter and the hunted, wolf tracks and caribou antlers add dimension and mystery to Arctic Alaska: The wolf is somewhere, and could be anywhere.*

*PRECEDING PAGES: Nothing in Alaska's Brooks Range stands out more impressively than the granitic, ice-wrought Arrigetch Peaks, in Gates of the Arctic National Park. FOLLOWING PAGES: At midnight in June, the turbid Jago River flows north from the Brooks Range, in Alaska's 19-million-acre Arctic National Wildlife Refuge.*

"This sense
of
independence
which it
gave was
second only to
the sense
of perfect
beauty..."

—ROBERT MARSHALL
*ALASKA WILDERNESS*

*M*aster of the northern skies,
the gyrfalcon makes its
year-round home from western
and northern Alaska, across
Canada, even as far east as
Greenland, preying chiefly on
other birds—in Alaska,
ptarmigan. The plumage of this
heavily built raptor varies from
white (see painting by John
James Audubon, page 35) to
mottled and very dark.

> "I was
> happy in the
> immediate
> presence
> of nature
> in its most
> staggering
> grandeur,
> in living
> intimately with
> something so
> splendidly
> immense...."

—ROBERT MARSHALL
*ALASKA WILDERNESS*

*In Alaska's high country, a Dall lamb walks over its tolerant mother's back (above). Jago River (right) braids through the Brooks Range toward the coastal plain of Alaska's Arctic National Wildlife Refuge.*

$A$laskan bull moose, North America's largest members of the deer family, each weighing

*more than a thousand pounds, battle for dominance during the autumn rut.*

"The
enjoyment
of solitude
...and
the beauty
of undefiled
panoramas
is absolutely
essential to
happiness."

—ROBERT MARSHALL
*ARCTIC VILLAGE*

*The Great Kobuk
Sand Dunes, covering
25 square miles above
the Arctic Circle,
spill to the edge
of Kavet Creek and
a spruce forest (left),
brightened here and
there by pioneering
plants, such as this
Siberian aster (below)
in Alaska's Kobuk
Valley National Park.*

# "No sight or sound or smell or feeling even remotely hinted of men or their creations."

—ROBERT MARSHALL
*ALASKA WILDERNESS*

A tundra swan, formerly called whistling swan (right), arrives to breed in the Arctic, a land bathed in light in summer, locked in darkness in winter. Sevisok Slough (below) meanders through Alaska's Noatak National Preserve. At 6.5 million acres, it ranks as the largest mountain-fringed wilderness river system in North America.

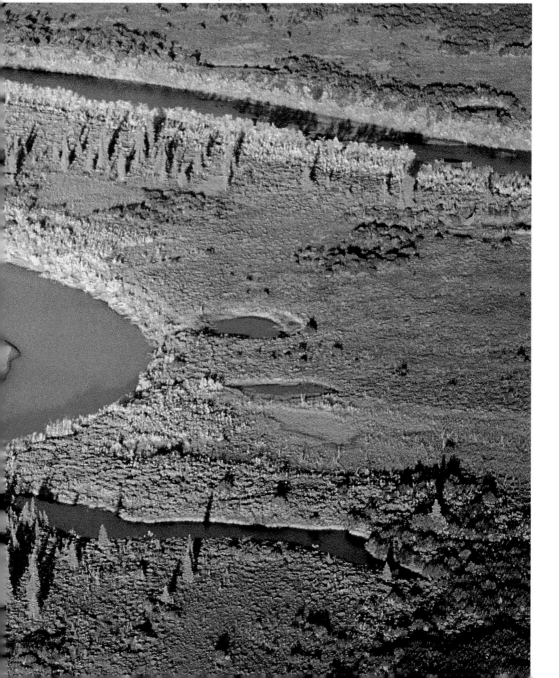

*A shoulder of Mount Marcy rises amid New York's Adirondacks, where Bob Marshall tested his mettle as a young man. Marshall, like Muir before him in the Sierra Nevada, would climb skyward to greet a howling storm and feel its energy surge into him.*

*FOLLOWING PAGES: Near the North Fork of the Sun River in "the Bob," the Bob Marshall Wilderness Area in Montana, a horseman rides in splendid autumn solitude.*

"In the whole vast panorama visible from the mountain there is virtually not a sign of civilization. Whichever way you look...there are the forests, the mountains, the ponds...."

—ROBERT MARSHALL, *THE HIGH PEAKS OF THE ADIRONDACKS*

# SOMETHING
# INFINITELY HEALING

# Rachel Carson and the House of Life

"What is the value of preserving and strengthening this sense of awe and wonder, this recognition of something beyond the boundaries of human existence? Is the exploration of the natural world just a pleasant way to pass the golden hours of childhood or is there something deeper?"

Rachel Carson, the scientist and writer who changed the world with a single book, answered her own question.

"I am sure there is something much deeper, something lasting and significant. Those who dwell, as scientists or laymen, among the beauties and mysteries of the earth are never alone or weary of life. Whatever the vexations or concerns of their personal lives, their thoughts can find paths that lead to inner contentment and to renewed excitement in living. Those who contemplate the beauty of the earth find reserves of strength that will endure as long as life lasts. There is symbolic as well as actual beauty in the migration of the birds, the ebb and flow of the tides, the folded bud ready for the spring. There is something infinitely healing in the repeated refrains of nature—the assurance that dawn comes after night, and spring after winter."

Healing was important to Rachel Carson.

In the summer of 1963 she went to her cottage on the Maine coast for the final time. Her 11-year-old grandnephew, Roger, joined her. He delighted in discovering limpet shells and gull feathers and bringing them to her. She listened to the music of birds, the symphony of the surf. The days were warm, the nights cool, the air fresh enough to assuage the pain from the cancer that was killing her. She had told no one of her illness outside a close circle of friends. "I'm going to say I have arthritis," she'd responded to the doctors upon hearing the bad news. "People don't dither at you so if you say you have arthritis. I will not have people dithering over me."

One year earlier, in June 1962, the *New Yorker* had published the first of three installments of her newest and most profound book.

"There was once a town in the heart of America where all life seemed to live in harmony with its surroundings," began her first chapter, "A Fable

*Ospreys, such as this one nesting in Maine, have prospered, as many bird species have, since the U.S. banned the application of DDT.*

*PRECEDING PAGES: On North Carolina's shore, gentle surf belies the sea's power, as Rachel Carson's quiet personality masked the power of her prose.*

for Tomorrow." It spoke to Everyman, Everywoman, every father and son, and mother and daughter. Readers by the millions fell into it with unsuspecting innocence, for it was not a fable at all but a terrible truth. America was being poisoned, and Rachel Carson had sounded the alarm.

"The town lay in the midst of a checkerboard of prosperous farms," she continued, "with fields of grain and hillsides of orchards where, in spring, white clouds of bloom drifted above the green fields. In autumn, oak and maple and birch set up a blaze of color that flamed and flickered across a backdrop of pines. Then foxes barked in the hills and deer silently crossed the fields, half hidden in the mists of the fall mornings."

Birds sang in dozens of dialects, and fish filled the rivers and streams. It had been this way as long as anybody could remember.

"Then a strange blight crept over the area and everything began to change." Farm animals began to die. Families fell ill. Plants withered and the birds quieted. "It was a spring without voices," Carson wrote. "On the mornings that had once throbbed with the dawn chorus of robins, catbirds, doves, jays, wrens, and scores of other bird voices there was now no sound; only silence lay over the fields and woods and marsh....No witchcraft, no enemy action had silenced the rebirth of new life in this stricken world. The people had done it themselves."

Thus began Rachel Carson's indictment of pesticides and herbicides and of the powerful industries that produced and promoted them. A single woman with a typewriter and a love for all living things would challenge corporate America—and win. She was an accomplished scientist and writer, a winner of the National Book Award, and the author of previous armchair hardcovers that had topped bestseller lists. But this book was different. It carried an extremely urgent message.

She called it *Silent Spring.*

"This town does not actually exist," she cautioned, "but it might easily have a thousand counterparts in America or elsewhere in the world. I know of no community that has experienced all the misfortunes I describe. Yet every one of these disasters has actually happened somewhere, and many real communities have already suffered a substantial number of them. A grim specter has crept upon us almost unnoticed, and this imagined tragedy may easily become a stark reality we all shall know."

For some 300 pages, in case study after case study, Carson carefully and eloquently described how dangerous chemicals could and would destroy not just unwanted insects and plants, but the entire ecology—the house of life—that sustains and includes every one of us. The destruction might be slow, and therefore be all the more insidious, and it would be inevitable unless we changed our ways.

"No conventional scientific study, however hair-raising its conclusions," wrote her editor and biographer, Paul Brooks, "could be expected to arouse such widespread interest. Rachel's genius lay in her ability to make a formidable subject like chlorinated hydrocarbons into a work of literature."

She did her research thoroughly and wanted the facts to speak for themselves, which they did. Equally if not more shocking were her anecdotes. She related two told to her by scientific observers of a Japanese beetle eradication program in Illinois. The first was about a dying meadowlark: "Although it lacked muscular coordination and could not fly or stand, it continued to beat its wings and clutch with its toes while lying on its side. Its beak was held open and breathing was labored." The second described a dead squirrel with its back arched, legs drawn into its body, toes clenched, and mouth filled with dirt that the dying animal had been biting at.

All organisms die; Carson was dying herself, but her deep moral, fiber told her none should die like this. "By acquiescing in an act that can cause such suffering to a living creature," she implored, "who among us is not diminished as a human being?... The question is whether any civilization can wage relentless war on life without destroying itself, and without losing the right to be called civilized."

She boldly concluded that "the 'control of nature' is a phrase conceived in arrogance, born of the Neanderthal age of biology and philosophy, when it was supposed that nature exists for the convenience of man. The... practices of applied entomology for the most part date from that Stone Age of science. It is our alarming misfortune that so primitive a science has armed itself with the most modern and terrible weapons, and that in turning them against the insects it has also turned them against the earth."

The storm she created was immediate and fierce, including parodies and personal attacks on that "hysterical woman" and "nun of nature." *Time* labeled the book an "emotional and inaccurate outburst." Nutrition and chemical organizations distributed a gaggle of unfavorable reviews that judged her work as polemic, not scientific, including one from the School of Public Health at Harvard University that called *Silent Spring* "baloney." Added the chief horticulturist at Michigan State University: "Her book is more poisonous than the pesticides she condemns."

All this while she was gravely ill.

Yet she appeared on national television, and like St. Francis of Assisi faced her dogmatic detractors with a gentle stoicism and love for nature that only exasperated them more. Even the American Medical Association clucked its displeasure. After all, the man who'd discovered the insecticidal properties of DDT had won the Nobel Prize. The debate was more than industry versus nature; it was dominion versus harmony, man versus woman. Nearly every attacker was a man who misjudged Carson's sunshine for shadow, her vision for blindness, her intellect for arrogance.

Paul Brooks observed: "The fury with which the book and its author were attacked had, I believe, deeper roots than the chemical companies' concern for profits. After all, DDT and other pesticides were not a vital part of their business. Her attackers must have realized that she was questioning not simply the use of poisons, but the basic irresponsibility of our industrial society toward the natural world: the belief that damage to nature was an inevitable cost of 'progress.' That was her heresy."

And her brilliance. Illumination comes from those who differ rather than agree with the prevailing order.

Secretary of the Interior Stewart L. Udall supported her. President Kennedy appointed a pesticides committee that in time would validate her. Supreme Court Justice William O. Douglas called *Silent Spring* "the most important chronicle of this century...." Translated and published around the world, it prompted Britain's Prince Philip to say: "I strongly recommend Rachel Carson's *Silent Spring* if you want to see what is going on."

Thirty years later Vice President Al Gore, a committed environmentalist, would have a photograph of Rachel Carson in his office and write,

"*Silent Spring* came as a cry in the wilderness, a deeply felt, thoroughly researched, and brilliantly written argument that changed the course of history. Without this book, the environmental movement might have been long delayed or never have developed at all."

Charles Darwin, a little more than a century earlier, had retreated to Down House after turning the world upside down—or right side up—with *The Origin of Species.* Rachel Carson did much the same, but despite her ill health remained in the fray as much as her strength allowed. The pain was constant now. She needed to relax in her cottage on a cliff above a wild shore. She had not only breast cancer but also heart problems. Some nights she went to sleep wondering if she would ever wake up. She kept her binoculars on her lap, ready for her best medicine of all: the angelic flights of terns, the flitting of a nearby nuthatch, the patient pose of a great blue heron. She shared her discoveries with young Roger, and he shared his with her.

"If a child is to keep alive his inborn sense of wonder without any such gift from the fairies," Rachel wrote in *Woman's Home Companion* (later reprised in the book, *The Sense of Wonder,* published after her death), "he needs the companionship of at least one adult who can share it, rediscovering with him the joy, excitement and mystery of the world we live in.…I sincerely believe that for the child, and for the parent seeking to guide him, it is half so important to *know* as to *feel.* If facts are the seeds that later produce knowledge and wisdom, then the emotions and the impressions of the senses are the fertile soil in which the seeds must grow. The years of early childhood are the time to prepare the soil."

Fifty years earlier, that soil and sense of wonder had been prepared for Rachel by her mother, Maria, a musical and bookish woman, who took her younger daughter for explorations in the woods as soon as she could walk. Rachel would whisper good morning to the birds as they sang their dawn chorus of twitters and trills. She felt the birds were answering her. This child's magic was easily nurtured in the rolling hills of western Pennsylvania, where Rachel was born in 1907. She was reared on a farm along the Allegheny River some 20 miles northeast of Pittsburgh. Cows, horses, and chickens interested her only a fraction the amount that woods, streams, and ponds did, where birds, insects, and reptiles lived. She read incessantly and at ten years of age wrote a story she submitted to a children's magazine, *St. Nicholas.* Summer came and went as she opened each new monthly issue to search for her story. By September it seemed hopeless, so she shrieked with glee when that month's issue arrived with her story inside. It won the Silver Badge. "I doubt that any royalty check of recent years has given me as great joy as the notice of that award," she commented decades later. This early success cemented a resolve. Carson, not yet a teenager, announced to her family that she would become a writer.

She was a quiet student, "noticed at school more by her teachers than by her classmates," according to Paul Brooks, and "imbued by her mother with intellectual ambition and a sense of her own worth rather than a desire for social success." Books were her closest companions.

She traveled the world on the words of John Masefield, Joseph Conrad, Herman Melville, Henry Williamson, and Henry Beston, great writers who filled her sails with the most mysterious of earthly realms— the sea. Even the less-than-literary *Coast Pilots and Sailing Directions,* published by the Government Printing Office, intrigued her. "Many of the descriptions of dangerous reefs and forbidding shores might almost have come out of Conrad," she wrote. "There is the sense of the sea's power and its capacity for doing the unexpected. And there is always the reminder of how little we know, and of the mystery that is eternally the sea's."

This would become her greatest romance: a love for the natural world with its distant shores and darkening depths and wondrously adapted creatures that by existence alone deserved their place on earth—a Magna Carta for all living things.

She entered Pennsylvania College for Women (now Chatham College) to pursue a degree in English but switched to zoology when an exciting teacher opened her eyes to science and natural history. She graduated magna cum laude, then earned a master's degree in zoology with emphasis in genetics from Johns Hopkins University. Years later when pesticide industry spokesmen belittled *Silent Spring,* saying that Rachel Carson was not a trained biologist, Paul Brooks, ever her bulldog—as Thomas Henry Huxley had been Darwin's—suggested they be "reserved a special corner in the Library of Hell, equipped with a barnacle-covered bench and a whale-oil lamp, by whose light they would be compelled to read out loud from her master's thesis: 'The Development of the Pronephros During the Embryonic and Early Larval Life of the Catfish (*Inctalurus punctatus*).'"

For several joyous summers she studied at the Woods Hole Marine Biological Laboratory in Massachusetts. The sea was everything she'd imagined: magical, mysterious, poetic, defiant. She marveled at the tidal currents surging to and fro, the angry waves breaking their backs on unsorry shores, the cornucopia of creatures in a plankton tow, the daily dramas of intertidal survival among echinoderms, mollusks, and crustaceans. How exciting it was to know so little about so much, to stand on the edge of a hidden, earthly universe. To have at your disposal an oceanography library among the world's best....No wonder the young scholar from Pennsylvania spent hundreds of hours there, reading and writing. She was in paradise.

She submitted one manuscript after another to literary magazines and watched her stack of rejection slips grow. Her persistence never flagged, however, and in the mid-1930s the Baltimore Sunday *Sun* published a series of feature articles she wrote on fisheries and related themes. During that same time her father died, and then her older sister, who left behind two elementary-school-age daughters to be brought up by Rachel and her mother. Though Rachel Carson would never marry or have children of her own, she would be a caregiver the rest of her life. She was employed part-time by the Bureau of Fisheries, writing radio broadcasts for the program *Romance Under the Waters.* But with the new burden of two orphaned nieces and an aging, widowed mother, she needed a steady job. The position of junior aquatic biologist opened up. She applied (the only woman who did), earned the highest score on the employment exam, and got the job.

When asked by her supervisor to write "something of a general sort" as an introduction to a booklet on the ocean for the commissioner of fisheries, Carson created a paean to the sea. Her supervisor smiled, handed it back to her, and said, "I don't think it will do. Better try again. But send this one to the *Atlantic Monthly.*"

She did. In September 1937, 20 years after announcing that she would be a writer, Carson's essay "Undersea" appeared in the *Atlantic Monthly.*

*FOLLOWING PAGES: Periwinkles, barnacles, and seaweed form an intertidal montage on the Maine coast, where Rachel Carson spent the last 11 summers of her life in a cottage above Sheepscot Bay.*

"Who has known the ocean?" she began. "Neither you nor I, with our earth-bound senses, know the foam and surge of the tide that beats over the crab hiding under the seaweed of his tide-pool home; or the lilt of the long, slow swells of mid-ocean, where shoals of wandering fish prey and are preyed upon, and the dolphin breaks the waves to breathe the upper atmosphere. Nor can we know the vicissitudes of life on the ocean floor, where the sunlight, filtering through a hundred feet of water, makes but a fleeting, bluish twilight, in which dwell sponge and mollusk and starfish and coral, where swarms of diminutive fish twinkle through the dusk like a silver rain of meteors, and eels lie in wait among the rocks. Even less is it given to man to descend those six incomprehensible miles into the recesses of the abyss, where reign utter silence and unvarying cold and eternal night."

Ears twitched, eyes blinked. New York's literati wondered: Who was this woman—this biologist, naturalist, essayist, and poet who so smoothly transmuted sea into sky? Who bridged the worlds of nature as an ambassador might the nations of men? A prodigy perhaps. Not long after "Undersea" appeared, Carson was contacted by an editor at a major publishing house. Would she like to write a book?

It was arduous work, done mostly at night after a long day in the office, where things were stressful since the Bureau of Fisheries had merged with the Biological Survey to form the Fish and Wildlife Service. Her two Persian cats slept on her lap and table while she wrote. Her mother, now 70, helped type the final draft and get it to the publisher on time—the last day of December 1940. *Under the Sea Wind* was released on the eve of Pearl Harbor. The world received her book with what she later called "superb indifference." Fewer than 1,600 copies sold in seven years, earning her less than a thousand dollars. She intended never to write another book.

"Never" turned out to be ten years.

While ascending the ranks of the U.S. Civil Service, from aquatic biologist to information specialist to chief editor of Fish and Wildlife Service publications, Carson quietly and methodically began to plan another book—not what she called just "another 'introduction to oceanography,'" but a definitive work on the sea. It was already within her, this masterpiece, as Michelangelo would say of his sculptures; all she needed to do was chip away the surrounding stone. Routine for a genius, and more, for although Carson was modest in her manner, she possessed strong confidence and a rare ability to synthesize an archipelago of scattered research—theses, dissertations, professional papers, raw statistics—into a single island of vivid prose that everyone could enjoy. The result was *The Sea Around Us,* her second book, published in July 1951.

Critics loved it. Accolades poured in from everywhere, not the least of which came from the great naturalists Edwin Way Teale and William Beebe, the explorer Thor Heyerdahl, and other members of prestigious scientific circles. Sales skyrocketed. *The Sea Around Us* topped the *New York Times* best-seller list in September, and by Christmas it was selling 4,000 copies a day. It would remain a best-seller for 86 weeks and eventually would be published in 32 languages around the world.

America had discovered Rachel Carson. She was honored and horrified. What was a shy woman to do with this beast called fame?

Accepting the National Book Award in 1952, she softly said, "If there is poetry in my book about the sea, it is not because I deliberately put it

"The face of the sea is always changing. ...Mysterious in the twilight, its aspects and its moods vary hour by hour...."

—RACHEL CARSON
*THE SEA AROUND US*

there, but because no one could write truthfully about the sea and leave out the poetry." She spoke of the many letters she had received from readers who found her book an antidote to "the stress and strain of human problems....Such letters make me wonder if we have not too long been looking through the wrong end of the telescope. We have looked first at man with his vanities and greed, and at his problems of a day or a year; and then only, and from this biased point of view, we have looked outward at the earth and at the universe of which our earth is so minute a part. Yet these are the great realities, and against them we see our human problems in a new perspective. Perhaps if we reversed the telescope and looked at man down these long vistas, we should find less time and inclination to plan for our own destruction."

The implication was obvious. Because we now had the ability to split atoms, manufacture toxins, and cause mass destruction anywhere on earth, did that give us the right? Ingenuity was one thing; wisdom another. Mankind had never been so dangerous or vulnerable. It was a difficult time for a woman of conscience. The birth of Rachel Carson as the quiet crusader had begun, and even she could not foresee the stature of her own potential—the full measure of what she would one day achieve.

She received honorary doctorates in science and literature, as well as many other awards, including the John Burroughs Medal for excellence in natural history writing. Her first book was re-released and quickly joined *The Sea Around Us* to create a publishing phenomenon: two simultaneous nonfiction best-sellers by the same author. It was gratifying, but Carson's finest moments remained those on sea and shore, wearing out the seat of her pants on the edges of tide pools on the Maine coast or kicking off her shoes on the sandy beach of North Carolina's Outer Banks. She remembered a day in Florida's upper Keys when she and a friend were standing at a bus stop, waiting to go to a yacht basin, their faces flushed with anticipation, arms filled with oceanography gear. A man walked by and smiled at them: "You girls look as though you're going out to discover a new world."

Indeed. That world was the ocean, where Rachel Carson would lose herself "getting acquainted with a whole village of sea anemones, crabs and so on...wading around in water up to my knees, not a human soul in sight."

Royalties from *The Sea Around Us* enabled her to resign from the Fish and Wildlife Service and build a summer cottage above Maine's Sheepscot Bay. She could write full-time now and was already at work on another book.

Whereas *The Sea Around Us* had largely addressed the physical aspects of the ocean, this next one would complement it, she explained, "by telling something of the story of how that marvelous, tough, vital, and adaptable something we know as LIFE has come to occupy one part of the sea world and how it has adjusted itself and survived despite the immense, blind forces acting upon it from every side."

*The Edge of the Sea* was published in 1955 and garnered more fame and awards for its author. Yet she shied away from society's firmament, devoting herself instead to unselfish hours caring for her mother and her niece, Marjorie, both of whom lived with her and were seriously ill.

She had many literary projects in mind. The choice was hers. Whatever she created would be a success; her stature ensured it. But in January 1958 the *Boston Herald* published a letter that sealed her fate.

The letter came from Olga Owens Huckins, a former newspaper writer whose hometown and private bird sanctuary north of Cape Cod had been sprayed with DDT by a mosquito-control plane. "The 'harmless' shower bath killed seven of our lovely songbirds outright," Huckins wrote. "We picked up three dead bodies the next morning right by the door. They were birds that had lived close to us, trusted us, and built their nests in our trees year after year. The next day three were scattered around the bird bath. (I had emptied it and scrubbed it after the spraying but YOU CAN NEVER KILL DDT)....Air spraying where it is not needed or wanted is inhuman, undemocratic, and probably unconstitutional. For those of us who stand helplessly on the tortured earth, it is intolerable."

Huckins sent a copy of the letter to her famous friend, Rachel Carson.

She was shocked. As far back as 1945 Carson had frowned when the miracle poison DDT, so useful in the malarial wartime tropics, was approved by the War Production Board for application by civilians in postwar America. Many government agencies sampled it, including, to her chagrin, her own: the Fish and Wildlife Service. She'd queried the *Reader's Digest* about the dangers of pesticides but received no positive response. Now, 13 years later, mass sprayings were being proposed. Augmenting Huckins's story was a 1957 DDT drenching of Long Island, ostensibly to eradicate the gypsy moth that, instead, showered dairy farms, fish ponds, salt marshes, even commuters at train stations and children at play. A quarter horse drank from a trough the planes had sprayed and ten hours later died. The incident prompted a court case with mountains of research and indignation. This time Rachel and her literary agent, Marie Rodell, proposed investigative stories on pesticides to four prestigious magazines. All four turned them down. "We doubt whether many of the things outlined in this letter could be substantiated," responded one editor, adding that he was "very dubious."

America in the 1950s was no model of social rebellion. Industry and orthodoxy said science would never create a problem it could not solve. Rachel Carson disagreed and traveled the untrodden path to say so: She wrote a book. It required four years of painstaking research, fact checking, and interviews. Her niece died; her mother died. She adopted Roger, her niece's son; and she was diagnosed with cancer. Yet still she worked, often to the edge of collapse. One night as she was finishing the last chapter, William Shawn, the editor of the *New Yorker*, called to say he'd read more than half and had been deeply touched. The book would succeed. Suddenly the tension of four years flooded out of her. She took her cat into her study, put a Beethoven violin concerto on the record player, and cried.

Carson chose these lines from a poem by John Keats for the book's half-title page:

> The sedge is wither'd from the lake,
> And no birds sing.

"What was this book which created such an uproar?" asked the *Audubon* magazine field editor, Frank Graham. "*Silent Spring* is, essentially, an ecological book. Almost everything that had been said about chemical pesticides before this time had been phrased in *economic* terms: we need more and better pesticides to grow bigger and better crops to make agriculture more profitable and more convenient for the farmer....Rachel

Carson approached the subject from a different direction—from the breadth of her experience in the biological sciences and the depth of her sympathy for all living things."

She supported Albert Schweitzer's "reverence for life" philosophy that declared man and nature to be inseparable, and she dedicated the book to him and his sobering prediction: "Man has lost the capacity to foresee and to forestall. He will end by destroying the earth."

Not an easy pill to swallow. But then came the words of Carson herself, the lyrical voice of the dying woman who loved birds and barnacles, even insects—"a group of extraordinarily varied and adaptable beings," of which she said a minuscule number competed with man for food. Should this justify their mass extermination? Sanction chemotherapy in the water, soil, and air? It was time to stop the folly, what Thomas Merton in a letter to Carson described as "our pitiful and superficial optimism about ourselves and our affluent society." Like Copernicus, Voltaire, and Muir, Carson gave us a simple message: The earth does not revolve around man any more than the sun revolves around the earth. She didn't advocate the elimination of all chemicals but rather "a determined and purposeful program of substitution, of replacing dangerous chemicals with new and even more efficient methods as rapidly as we can."

"So you're the little lady who started this whole thing," Abraham Lincoln said during the Civil War to Harriet Beecher Stowe, author of *Uncle Tom's Cabin.* A century later Rachel Carson appeared before Senator Abraham Ribicoff's committee amid another war—the one against environmental toxins. "Miss Carson," Ribicoff said, "you are the lady who started all this."

She visited Maine for her last summer and watched the fall migration of monarch butterflies, then returned to Maryland to close her life. Prestigious awards fell on her like rain: the Schweitzer Medal of the Animal Welfare Institute, the Conservationist of the Year Award from the National Wildlife Federation, a special commendation from the Garden Club of America. That organization had already acknowledged her with its highest conservation award, the Frances Hutchinson Medal. Years later, after her death, President Jimmy Carter would award her the Presidential Medal of Freedom.

While DDT and other harmful chlorinated hydrocarbons have been banned—saving the bald eagle, the peregrine falcon, the Atlantic salmon, and many other species from extinction—new and questionable pesticides are still being developed and marketed. In 1992, the same year a panel of distinguished Americans voted *Silent Spring* the most influential book of the last half century, 2.2 billion pounds of pesticides were used in the United States—eight pounds for every man, woman, and child. The war continues.

The lady who started it all asked to be pushed outside in her wheelchair one spring morning in 1964. She knew her time was short. She wanted to hear the warblers, chickadees, and kinglets and tell them goodbye.

She died a few days later on April 14, at age 56.

"For all at last return to the sea—to Oceanus, the ocean river, like the everflowing stream of time, the beginning and the end."

A wildlife refuge was named for her on the Maine coast. A postage stamp was dedicated to her. But no honor could match the tribute paid her when in 1979 a team of Fish and Wildlife Service biologists climbed onto the roof of the Interior Building in Washington, D.C., and released into the wild three healthy peregrine falcons. One of them was named Rachel.

"Knowing what I do, there would be no future peace for me if I kept silent.... It is, in the deepest sense, a privilege as well as a duty... to speak out— to many thousands of people...."

—RACHEL CARSON
*LETTER, JUNE 1958*

"I can
remember
no time
when
I wasn't
interested in
the...
whole world
of nature
...and spent
a great deal
of time
in woods
and beside
streams...."

—RACHEL CARSON
*SPEECH, APRIL 1954*

*All creatures, including this northern flying squirrel (top) and red squirrel
(above) deserve respect, according to Rachel Carson's world view, similar
to that of Albert Schweitzer. In Maine's Mahoosuc Range (opposite) runoff from
a recent rain swirls life-giving water through Step Falls Preserve.*

*PRECEDING PAGES: Chilly autumn fog envelopes a blueberry and
spruce bog in Maine's Acadia National Park.*

"There is always something new to discover and I never go down to the low tide world without a sense of anticipation."

—RACHEL CARSON
*SPEECH, MAY 1955*

*S*un stars (opposite) and other colorful, wondrous creatures of the intertidal zone delighted Rachel Carson and her grandnephew, Roger, as they often walked the beaches together. "...I believe children can be helped to hear the many voices about them," Carson observed. "Take time to listen and talk about the voices of the earth and what they mean—the majestic voice of thunder, the winds, the sound of surf or flowing streams." The eternal surf pounds ashore with no less fury and poetry now than before, striking the southern Maine coast (above) at what has been preserved as the Rachel Carson National Wildlife Refuge.

*P*icture of patience, a great egret waits, still as a stone, for an unsuspecting fish to

swim below, when—with lightning speed—it will impale the fish with its daggerlike bill.

"*The sight of these small living creatures…, fragile against the brute force of the sea, had moving philosophical overtones…," wrote Carson of ghost crabs (below). As would sea oats (opposite), pioneering amid wind and salt spray on North Carolina's coast.*

*FOLLOWING PAGES: Migrating snow geese burst skyward from a staging area at Cape Hatteras National Seashore in North Carolina.*

# "We should know…Nature's way…what the earth would have been had not man interfered."

—RACHEL CARSON, *HOLIDAY, JULY 1958*

# PARADOX AND BEDROCK

## PARADOX AND BEDROCK

# Edward Abbey
# and the Arid Truth

"For the first time I felt I was getting close to the West of my deepest imaginings—the place where the tangible and the mythical become the same." Seventeen-year-old Edward Abbey, fresh off his family farm in Pennsylvania and traveling penniless around America by boxcar, thumb, and bus, had found the sunstruck slickrock canyon country of the American Southwest. It was the summer of 1944, the season of D-Day. Allied forces were marching toward Berlin, and Abbey would soon turn 18 and be shipped off to Italy to serve in the Second World War. Among the visions he would carry with him: a memory of the desert as seen from a boxcar in New Mexico, as sustaining as a family photograph.

"Proud of my freedom and hobohood," he recalled years later, "I stood in the doorway of the boxcar, rocking with the motion of the train, ears full of the rushing wind and the clattering wheels, and stared and stared and stared, like a starving man, at the burnt, barren, bold, bright landscape passing before my eyes. Telegraph poles flashed by close to the tracks, the shining wires dipped and rose, dipped and rose; but beyond the line and the road and the nearby ridges, the queer foreign shapes of mesa and butte seemed barely to move at all; they revolved slowly at an immense distance, strange right-angled promontories of rose-colored rock that remained in view, from my slowly altering perspective, for an hour, for two hours, at a time. And all of it there, simply *there,* neither hostile nor friendly, but full of a powerful, mysterious promise."

The desert hadn't spoken to young Edward Abbey; it had whispered, its voice wondrously haunting and beguiling. Others might have found those "foreign shapes of mesa and butte" inscrutable or insignificant. They might not have seen or heard them at all. Many travelers before Abbey had in fact found the desert frightening, a loathsome place of suffering and death, an impediment—a place not to get to, but to get through. For a hundred years they had struggled beyond its parched arroyos and endless flats, its briny evaporites and bleached bones, to reach the golden shores of California and the verdant valleys of Oregon—the promised land. Eden.

*September sunset paints rock-ribbed walls above Granite Rapid on the Colorado River in the Inner Gorge of Arizona's Grand Canyon National Park.*

*PRECEDING PAGES: Summer storm boils over Entrada sandstone not far from where Abbey lived in his simple trailer, in Utah's Arches National Park.*

To them, the desert was a hell.

Many early maps of North America designated all lands west of the Mississippi River as "The Great American Desert." A wasteland. Contemporary dictionaries still describe deserts this way, meaning, in effect, they are waterless and unsuitable for human habitation. For Edward Abbey, nothing could have been more attractive: Here was a place the rest of the world had largely ignored. A place for him, his Walden, where he could practice the fine art of simplifying his life, just as Henry David Thoreau had done more than a century before. He would admire ravens, watch clouds, listen to wrens, and smell the sage after a spring storm.

Cactus Ed, people would call him, partly because of his whiskered chin, partly for his spiny disposition. But also, and most important, because under that rough exterior was a sensitive man who had fallen in love with the land; a man acutely alive, defiant as a cholla, yes, but able to blossom and celebrate being rooted in his new home—the desert.

"I want to be able to look at and into a juniper tree," he wrote, "a piece of quartz, a vulture, a spider, and see it as it is in itself, devoid of all humanly ascribed qualities, anti-Kantian, even the categories of scientific description. To meet God or Medusa face to face, even if it means risking everything human in myself. I dream of a hard and brutal mysticism in which the naked self merges with a nonhuman world and yet somehow survives still intact, individual, separate. Paradox and bedrock."

No ordinary man. No ordinary landscape.

Out of the military, Abbey returned to the West in 1948 to attend the University of New Mexico, in Albuquerque. He studied classical philosophy, chased girls, and wrote two early novels: *Jonathan Troy* and *The Brave Cowboy*. His most highly praised work was yet to come, however, and would be inspired by time in the wilderness in a then little-known place called Arches National Monument.

One day in late March 1956 Abbey loaded his meager belongings into his pickup truck in Albuquerque and drove 450 miles northwest to Moab, Utah, on the Colorado River. It was dark and windy when he arrived a short distance outside Moab at the entrance of Arches, where he was greeted by the superintendent and chief ranger, two of only three permanent employees at the monument. "After coffee," Abbey wrote, "they gave me a key to the housetrailer and directions on how to reach it; I am required to live and work not at headquarters but at this one-man station some twenty miles back in the interior, on my own. The way I wanted it, naturally, or I'd never have asked for the job."

He drove through the darkness and turned off the paved highway into terra incognita. "Wind roaring out of the northwest," he recalled, "black clouds across the stars—all I could see were clumps of brush and scattered junipers along the roadside." A wooden sign came into view:

WARNING: QUICKSAND
DO NOT CROSS WASH
WHEN WATER IS RUNNING

"The wash looked perfectly dry in my headlights. I drove down, across, up the other side and on into the night. Glimpses of weird humps of pale rock on either side, like petrified elephants, dinosaurs, stone-age hobgoblins. Now and then something alive scurried across the road: kangaroo mice, a jackrabbit, an animal that looked like a cross between a raccoon and a squirrel—the ringtail cat. Farther on a pair of mule deer started from the brush and bounded obliquely through the beams of my lights, raising puffs of dust which the wind, moving faster than my pickup truck, caught and carried ahead of me out of sight into the dark. The road...dipped in and out of tight ravines, climbing by degrees toward a summit which I would see only in the light of the coming day."

For 300 million years the processes that created the landscape of Abbey's dreams included accumulation of sediments in salty seas, along shorelines, in vast sand dunes, and beside rivers and streams. In later years faulting, uplifting, and erosion began creating this wonderland of rocks. Arches, like more than 20 other national parks and monuments, belongs to the Colorado Plateau, that region of Utah and Arizona characterized by stratified formations of sandstones, limestones, and shales. Only during the last 10 million years or so of erosion have most of the uppermost layers of rock been removed.

Originally flexed and warped by underground salt movement and pressure from overlying rocks into anticlines (long, cigar-shaped upfolds), the now exposed sandstones continued to rebound, causing even more fracturing and splintering of the relatively soft rock. Water seeped into cracks, froze, and flaked off pieces of the rock. Narrow fins formed. Oval-shaped slabs peeled away and opened windows into their flanks that enlarged into arches and the other phantasmagoric shapes—spires, temples, balanced rocks, and flying buttresses—that Abbey, on his first night here, saw as "weird humps of pale rock...."

Today, more than 2,000 stone spans punctuate the area. "These are natural arches," Abbey wrote, "holes in the rock, windows in stone, no two alike, as varied in form as in dimension." Some, such as Delicate Arch, express the near-perfect symmetry of middle age. Others are youthful windows. And at least one, Landscape Arch—a stone span 306 feet long, 92 feet above the ground, and only 12 feet thick at its center—shows extreme old age and could collapse any day. The same processes that create an arch—water, ice, differential erosion, the expansion of rock—will also tear it down.

Fins, windows, arches, hoodoos, spires, temples, and towers—there seems no end to it, and indeed there is not, for the rocks are only the beginning. Add to them an elegant mosaic of plant life, the liquid songs of birds, the immense open space, and it's no wonder Edward Abbey was seduced. Admiring it all the first morning after his arrival, he declared, "This is the most beautiful place on earth.

"There are many such places. Every man, every woman, carries in heart and mind the image of the ideal place, the right place, the one true home, known or unknown, actual or visionary. A houseboat in Kashmir, a view down Atlantic Avenue in Brooklyn, a gray gothic farmhouse...in the Allegheny Mountains, a cabin on the shore of a blue lake in spruce and fir country, a greasy alley near the Hoboken waterfront, or...for those of a less demanding sensibility, the world to be seen from a comfortable apartment high in the tender, velvety smog of Manhattan, Chicago, Paris, Tokyo, Rio or Rome—there's no limit to the human capacity for the homing sentiment. Theologians, sky pilots, astronauts have even felt the appeal of home calling to them from up above, in the cold black outback of interstellar space.

"For myself, I'll take Moab, Utah. I don't mean the town itself, of course,

"A landscape, like a man or woman, acquires character through time and endurance."

—EDWARD ABBEY
*A VOICE CRYING
IN THE WILDERNESS*

141

but the country which surrounds it—the canyonlands. The slickrock desert. The red dust and the burnt cliffs and the lonely sky—all that which lies beyond the end of the roads."

For two memorable seasons, April to October of 1956 and 1957, Abbey did just that; he worked as a ranger and lived on a dirt road in Arches National Monument, feeling, he wrote, "Loveliness and a quiet exultation."

Sitting one morning on the doorstep of his house trailer, ritually drinking his black coffee and facing the rising sun, he discovered a rattlesnake beneath him, almost between his bare feet, just behind his heels. "No mistaking that wedgelike head," he wrote, "that tip of horny segmented tail peeping out of the coils." Not a good situation, but not an unmanageable one. The morning was early; the motionless snake, torpid in the cool air. Abbey considered killing it; he had a revolver in the trailer. It was actually a variety of small rattlesnake called the faded midget. "An insulting name for a rattlesnake," he observed, "which may explain the Faded Midget's alleged bad temper. But the name is apt: he is small and dusty-looking, with a little knob above each eye—the horns."

Abbey weighed his options. "I finish my coffee, lean back and swing my feet up and inside the doorway of the trailer. At once there is a buzzing sound from below and the rattler lifts his head from his coils, eyes brightening, and extends his narrow black tongue to test the air."

Rather than shoot the snake, Ranger Abbey, whose duty, he reminded himself, was to "protect, preserve and defend all living things within the park boundaries," grabbed a long-handled spade and scooped the snake into the open. "He strikes; I can hear the click of the fangs against steel, see the stain of venom. He wants to stand and fight, but I am patient; I insist on herding him well away from the trailer."

About a week later the rattler returned, coiled beneath the trailer, ominous. Again Abbey considered killing it, but again did not. Later, a short distance away, he found a harmless gopher snake, which he knew was an adversary of the rattler. He captured it in a burlap bag and released it into his trailer, hoping it would reduce the surplus mouse population and displace the rattler.

Man and gopher snake shared an amicable relationship.

"When I take him outside into the wind and sunshine," Abbey recalled, "his favorite place seems to be inside my shirt, where he wraps himself around my waist and rests on my belt. In this position he sometimes sticks his head out between shirt buttons for a survey of the weather, astonishing and delighting any tourists who may happen to be with me at the time."

Turning the gopher snake loose on the sandstone around the trailer did indeed evict the rattler. Abbey was pleased. But one day when he returned from patrol, the gopher snake, like the rattler, was nowhere to be found. A month passed. "I'm in the stifling heat of the trailer," Abbey wrote, "opening a can of beer, barefooted, about to go outside and relax after a hard day watching cloud formations. I happen to glance out the little window near the refrigerator and see two gopher snakes on my verandah engaged in what seems to be a kind of ritual dance. Like a living caduceus they wind and unwind about each other in undulant, graceful, perpetual motion, moving slowly across a dome of sandstone."

Was it his old friend, the snake he had carried in his shirt? He couldn't tell. If so, it had returned with a mate.

Abbey went outside to watch them, welcome them; he crawled onto his belly and inched toward them.

"Obsessed with their ballet," he wrote, "the serpents seem unaware of my presence....I crawl after them, determined to see the whole thing. Suddenly and simultaneously they discover me, prone on my belly a few feet away. The dance stops. After a moment's pause the two snakes come straight toward me, still in flawless unison, straight toward my face, the forked tongues flickering, their intense wild yellow eyes staring directly into my eyes. For an instant I am paralyzed by wonder; then, stung by a fear too ancient and powerful to overcome I scramble back, rising to my knees. The snakes veer and turn and race away from me in parallel motion, their lean elegant bodies making a soft hissing noise as they slide over the sand and stone. I follow them for a short distance, still plagued by curiosity, before remembering my place and the requirements of common courtesy."

Abbey did not see the two gopher snakes again, or the rattler, yet he said he felt their presence watching over him, "like totemic deities." He made no apologies for anthropomorphism, and in fact questioned the prejudice that denied "any form of emotion to all animals but man and his dog."

With careful intensity he contemplated the world around him: the circular patterns made in the sand by wind-whipped wild grass, the tracks of tiger lizards and kangaroo rats, nature's "garden" of mule-ear sunflowers, Indian paintbrush, yellow borage, skyrocket gilia, scarlet penstemon—and the loveliest of all, cliff rose, "...sweet as a pretty girl," he wrote, "with a fragrance like that of orange blossoms." Also of special brilliance were the flowering cacti: prickly pear, hedgehog, and fishhook.

He apprenticed himself to a favorite juniper tree, hoping to learn from it, to intuit some higher meaning from its form, color, and texture—its static pose. He estimated it at 300 years old, a grandmother tree. Half of it was leafless and dead; the other half thrived and produced countless berries. That both life and death could dwell in the same organism was the kind of dichotomy that intrigued Edward Abbey. He himself could be irascible and tender, acidic and soothing, frail and strong—a dry, dusty compendium of antonyms scattered across the sandstone like desert seeds, hard on the outside, soft on the inside.

The Spanish bayonet, or yucca, a member of the lily family, was another Abbey favorite. "Despite its fierce defenses, or perhaps because of them," he wrote, "the yucca is as beautiful as it is strange, perfect in its place wherever that place may be—on the Dagger Flats of Big Bend, the high grasslands of southern New Mexico, the rim and interior of Grand Canyon or here in the Arches country, growing wide-spaced and solitaire from the red sands of Utah."

The same could be said of him.

Abbey was not a scientist, and proud of it; rather, he was a writer with a rare genius for extracting little lessons from the natural world around him, the daily dramas of night and day, predator and prey, order and chaos; with the ability to see open, silent places as tonic and teacher, and to frame it all with wit, humor, sarcasm, and satire.

Every lover of wilderness develops a certain measure of propriety, a caretaker's instincts, for his or her own sacred ground, especially in today's

*FOLLOWING PAGES: "The dory plunges down into the watery hole," wrote Abbey of Horn Creek Rapids on the Colorado River, "then up the slope of the standing wave. Water topples upon us, filling the boat in an instant. The force of the river carries us through the first wave and into a second, deeper hole...." For Abbey, as for thousands of others who have floated, paddled, and rowed the Colorado River through the Grand Canyon, no other experience could compare. Or needed to.*

BRUCE DALE

rapidly changing world where technologies take on lives and justifications of their own. Abbey felt this. He regarded Arches as a perfect place that could not be improved and that should never be trampled beneath the juggernaut of growth and progress. He embraced his desert as if it were an encore to a great performance, with the final curtain already closing. Man had destroyed pieces of every other biome on the planet, and Abbey feared his beloved desert, a last bastion of roadlessness, would be next.

When a thirsty three-man survey crew showed up at his trailer in a jeep one day, ready to stake a new paved road into the area, Abbey was horrified. The head man, a civil engineer, explained, "When this road is built you'll get ten, twenty, thirty times as many tourists in here as you get now. His men nodded in solemn agreement, and he stared at me intently, waiting to see what possible answer I could have to that.

" 'Have some more water,' I said. I had an answer all right but I was saving it for later. I knew I was dealing with a madman."

Roughly ten years later, after the new road was constructed, Abbey returned to Arches to find the engineer's words prophetic. "The Master Plan has been fulfilled," he wrote. "Where once a few adventurous people came on weekends to camp for a night or two and enjoy a taste of the primitive and remote, you will now find serpentine streams of baroque automobiles pouring in and out, all through the spring and summer....The little campgrounds where I used to putter around reading three-day-old newspapers full of lies and watermelon seeds have now been consolidated into one master campground that looks, during the busy season, like a suburban village: elaborate housetrailers of quilted aluminum crowd upon gigantic camper-trucks of Fiberglas and molded plastic; through their windows you will see the blue glow of television and hear the studio laughter of Los Angeles....

"Progress has come at last to the Arches, after a million years of neglect."

The growth didn't stop there. Annual visitation to Arches—a national park since 1971—grew from roughly 25,000 in 1957 to 777,000 in 1994, more than a 30-fold increase in 38 years. Other national parks in the American Southwest have annual visitations in the millions, as Arches probably will in the near future.

The bumpy, twisting dirt road Edward Abbey drove across Willow Flats to reach his trailer, near Balanced Rock, in the 1950s, is now a four-wheel drive track. A road supply depot occupies his old trailer site. The new paved road, with a posted speed limit of 45 mph, ends at Devils Garden Trailhead and parking lot, near the north end of the park. It's not uncommon to see cars or motor homes zooming along this road, or coasting through the parking lot with passengers videotaping nature through tinted windows.

Abbey saw it—or the beginnings of it—and howled with indignation. "No more cars in national parks," he proposed. "Let the people walk. Or ride horses, bicycles, mules, wild pigs—anything—but keep the automobiles and the motorcycles and all their motorized relatives out. We have agreed not to drive our automobiles into cathedrals, concert halls, art museums, legislative assemblies, private bedrooms and the other sanctums of our culture; we should treat our national parks with the same deference, for they, too, are holy places."

Every year thousands of people hike the popular Devils Garden Trail to see the arches named Landscape, Double O, Partition, Navajo, Private, and others. The trail is ten feet wide and nicely graveled in the beginning. The laughter of children can be heard, occasional running footsteps, people exclaiming their admiration as they pause reverently below the great spans of Entrada sandstone. A chipmunk may suddenly appear, or a lizard, pausing briefly before hurrying away to shelter, wary of kestrel and hawk. The peopleless silence Abbey loved, however, what he described as the "mighty stillness that embraces and includes me," can be difficult to find. The concert hall is getting crowded.

But drama and beauty still remain. Light and shadow still dance on the rocks. Great convection clouds still build on warm afternoons, sending lightning and thunder crackling over the land. Sudden rains still produce flash floods, the water, unable to seep into bare rock, flowing down, down, down with rivulet swelling to stream, stream to torrent, the entire turbid flood carrying away the sandstone grain by grain, cutting more wrinkles into the ancient, weathered face of the canyon country.

A small but important amount of the rainwater pools in natural bedrock depressions, called potholes. Buried in the silt, sand, and clay at the bottom of these depressions are the eggs of shrimp. Triggered by moisture and temperature, the eggs hatch and develop into adults that must complete their life cycles and lay the next generation of eggs before the ephemeral pools evaporate. Tadpoles develop as well, and soon leagues of toads hop across bare rock in search of insects. Elsewhere, far into the deepest, shadiest clefts of the canyons, cool grottos sustain hanging gardens of monkey flower, maidenhair fern, and orchid—islands of moisture in a sea of aridity. Nighttime, too, is an oasis, as many animals are most active then: the kangaroo rat, the ringtail cat, the moth pollinating the yucca, the bat pollinating the agave.

"Strolling on," Abbey celebrated, "it seems to me that the strangeness and wonder of existence are emphasized here, in the desert, by the comparative sparsity of the flora and fauna: life not crowded upon life as in other places but scattered abroad in sparseness and simplicity, with a generous gift of space..., so that the living organism stands out bold and brave and vivid against the lifeless sand and barren rock. The extreme clarity of the desert light is equaled by the extreme individuation of desert life-forms. Love flowers best in openness and freedom."

Abbey returned to Arches for a third season in the mid-1960s, and in 1968 his first book of essays, *Desert Solitaire,* was published and quietly released to a nation preoccupied with civil rights, the Vietnam War, and the Beatles. Hardly anyone heard the anarchist in the canyons. But Earth Day arrived; the environmental movement grew. And as it did, so did word about *Desert Solitaire.* It changed people's lives. They labeled it a classic as distinctly American as Thomas Paine's *Common Sense* and Mark Twain's *Huckleberry Finn.* Novelist Larry McMurtry called Abbey "the Thoreau of the American West."

The needle of Abbey's compass pointed to every southwestern desert: the Chihuahuan of New Mexico, the Sonoran of Arizona, the Mojave of California. Abbey explored them all. He paddled, rowed, and drifted down the Colorado River many times, once through Glen Canyon before it was drowned by Lake Powell, behind the dam that broke his heart.

"What draws us into the desert is the search for something intimate in the remote."

—EDWARD ABBEY
*A VOICE CRYING IN THE WILDERNESS*

"I take a dim view of dams," he mused. "I find it hard to learn to love cement; I am poorly impressed by concrete aggregates and statistics in the cubic tons. But in this weakness I am not alone, for I belong to that ever-growing number of Americans, probably a good majority now, who have become aware that a fully industrialized, thoroughly urbanized, elegantly computerized social system is not suitable for human habitation. Great for machines, yes. But unfit for people."

Abbey loved every wild hollow and furrow in the canyon country and angrily lamented every infraction upon them. His comic novel, *The Monkey Wrench Gang,* published in 1975, chronicled the escapades of four environmental desperadoes who sabotaged industrial equipment to save the West, ultimately setting their sights on the destruction of Glen Canyon Dam, to liberate the Colorado River. "He remembered the real Colorado," Abbey wrote of Seldom Seen Smith, a river guide and one of his four protagonists, "before damnation, when the river flowed unchained and unchanneled in the joyous floods of May and June, swollen with snow melt. Boulders crunching and clacking and grumbling, tumbling along on the river's bedrock bed, the noise like that of grinding molars in a giant jaw. That was a river."

*The Monkey Wrench Gang* spawned a new breed of environmental activism and, together with *Desert Solitaire* and subsequent books of essays, elevated Abbey to the status of hero. His editor, John Macrae, wrote: "By 1980 Ed Abbey had become a literary divine, like it or not." But he was still an iconoclast. When the Academy of Arts and Letters offered him a major prize in 1986, Abbey refused, saying, "It's too late. Besides, prizes are for little boys."

So, too, he believed, was the cowboy mystique. In April 1985 he delivered an incendiary speech at the University of Montana—the heart of cattle country—saying that Western ranchers should no longer be allowed to raise their cattle on public lands. These lands were not just overgrazed, he said; they were "cowburnt." His solution: Shoot the cattle, stop the government subsidy, and give the lands back to the original inhabitants: the elk, moose, buffalo, eagle. Such blasphemy had been whispered before but never proclaimed. To preface the speech, Abbey pulled a .44 revolver from his briefcase, waved it around, and set it on the lectern, saying "When I finish this little talk I'd be glad to answer any questions you might have."

The speech was published in *Harper's* magazine and as a chapter in his book of essays *One Life at a Time, Please.* Abbey lost friends over it. When asked if tempering his style might be more constructive, he replied, "No…I've been willing to be dismissed as a crank and a crackpot simply for the pleasure of saying exactly what I really do believe."

"It is my belief," he wrote in his essay "A Writer's Credo," "that the writer, the freelance author, should be and must be a critic of the society in which he lives." He postulated that truth is the enemy of power, as power is the enemy of truth. He explored the writer's "duty to speak the truth—especially unpopular truth. Especially truth that offends the powerful, the rich, the well-established, the traditional, the mythic, the sentimental. To attack, when the time makes it necessary, the sacred cows of his society." From cattle ranchers on public lands, to growth-addicted chambers of commerce, to the apocalyptic urbanism of Las Vegas, few infractions on wild America escaped Abbey's predatory pen.

Though diagnosed with a life-threatening condition in 1982, he had continued to write, telling only his family and close friends of his sickness. He traveled back to Pennsylvania and wrote what he called his "fat masterpiece," a partly autobiographical novel entitled *The Fool's Progress*. After that came a final novel, *Hayduke Lives!* the long-awaited sequel to *The Monkey Wrench Gang*, which he finished shortly before dying on March 14, 1989, at his Tucson, Arizona, home at the age of 62.

"The plow of mortality drives through the stubble, turns over rocks and sod and weeds to cover the old, the worn-out, the husks, shells, empty seedpods and sapless roots, clearing the field for the next crop. A ruthless, brutal process—but clean and beautiful."

Some 30 years earlier Ranger Abbey had been part of a search party that found a dead tourist on Grand View Point, in today's Canyonlands National Park, near Arches. Apparently overwhelmed by the summer heat, the man had crawled under a juniper and suffered heart failure. "Looking out on this panorama of light, space, rock and silence," Abbey wrote, "I am inclined to congratulate the dead man on his choice of jumping-off place; he had good taste. He had good luck—I envy him the manner of his going: to die alone, on rock under sun at the brink of the unknown, like a wolf, like a great bird, seems to me very good fortune indeed. To die in the open, under the sky, far from the insolent interference of leech and priest, before this desert vastness opening like a window onto eternity—that surely was an overwhelming stroke of rare good luck."

Abbey accepted his own death as he did life—with uncommon honesty. No regrets. Friends fulfilled his wish and carried his body into the desert to leave him where he could fertilize a cliff rose or cactus. Reincarnate into a vulture. He wanted no funeral, but rather a wake with music, singing, dancing, and storytelling. He got two of them: one outside Tucson, the other outside Arches National Park.

The anarchist who distilled his philosophy from the dry desert air was gone, but he left behind 21 books. He was married five times, and he fathered five children. His readers remember the public Abbey: angry, passionate, sarcastic, ardently jousting with the juggernauts of industrialism—"growth for the sake of growth is the ideology of the cancer cell"—but those who knew him personally remember the private Abbey: kind, sensitive, a cherished friend, a good husband, a loving father.

Though Arches National Park has changed since Abbey worked there, to reach Delicate Arch, icon of the park, still requires a three-mile round-trip pilgrimage by foot over sunburnt Entrada sandstone, past piñons and junipers amid what Abbey called "the sense of *waiting* that seems to hover in the air." The pilgrims climb higher, walk a ledge, round a corner and there it is: Delicate Arch, improbably perfect, a ring of stone set on the far side of a natural amphitheater filled with amber light. A few admirers fidget with their cameras; most sit in silence and awe.

"A weird, lovely, fantastic object out of nature like Delicate Arch," Abbey wrote, " has the curious ability to remind us—like rock and sunlight and wind and wilderness—that *out there* is a different world, older and greater and deeper by far than ours....For a few moments we discover that nothing can be taken for granted, for if this ring of stone is marvelous then all which shaped it is marvelous, and our journey here on earth, able to see and touch and hear in the midst of tangible and mysterious things-in-themselves, is the most strange and daring of all adventures."

"In recording my impressions of the natural scene I have striven above all for accuracy, since I believe that there is a kind of poetry... in simple fact."

—EDWARD ABBEY
*DESERT SOLITAIRE*

$S$ymmetry and a prickly beauty dwell in the desert amid the whorled leaves and barbs of an agave (below), in a yucca (opposite), and in the desert scorpion. The yucca's flowers, Abbey observed, were "pollinated not by bees or hummingbirds but exclusively by a moth of the genus Pronuba...." Deserts, with their sharp and sometimes painful beauty, spoke an arid truth to Abbey, whose barbed prose defended them and the life they held, like the scorpion, against transgressors, large or small.

PRECEDING PAGES: Winter patina of fresh snow captures sunrise from Mather Point on the South Rim of the Grand Canyon.

"Our world is so full of beautiful things: Fruit and ideas and woman and banjo music and onions with purple skins."

—EDWARD ABBEY
*EVERY RIVER I TOUCH TURNS TO HEARTBREAK*

"Not the work of a cosmic hand, nor sculptured by sand-bearing winds, as many people prefer to believe," wrote Abbey, "the arches came into being and continue to come into being through the modest wedging action of rainwater, melting snow, frost, and ice, aided by gravity. In color they shade from off-white through buff, pink, brown and red, tones which also change with the time of day and the moods of the light, the weather, the sky." Among the most fantastic: Landscape Arch, at 306 feet one of the longest sandstone arches in the world (above), and North and South Windows, also called the Spectacles, both in Utah's Arches National Park, home to more than 2,000 natural stone spans.

"It is not enough to understand the natural world; the point is to defend and preserve it."

—EDWARD ABBEY
*A VOICE CRYING IN THE WILDERNESS*

*With antediluvian cunning, a collared lizard seizes a lunch of darkling beetle. Reptiles find the desert habitable; their body temperatures rise and fall with the warm days and cool nights, concentrating energy when necessary and conserving it when not.*

"...bold and brave and vivid against...the barren rock."

—EDWARD ABBEY, *DESERT SOLITAIRE*

*Symbol of the Sonoran Desert, a saguaro lifts its gigantic arms into the southern Arizona sky (opposite), cradling clusters of flowers as high as 60 feet above the ground (right) and a family of nesting great horned owls. The flowers are pollinated at night by long-nosed bats and during the day by insects.*

*FOLLOWING PAGES: Spring in Organ Pipe Cactus National Monument finds Mexican gold poppies splashed amid a cholla cactus skeleton.*

JOHN CANCALOSI/DRK PHOTO; GEORGE H.H. HUEY (TOP); PAT O'HARA (LEFT); WILLARD CLAY (FOLLOWING PAGES)

"...extreme individuation of desert life-forms. Love flowers best in openness and freedom."

—EDWARD ABBEY, *DESERT SOLITAIRE*

*Pools of water become pools of life—aquatic islands in a sea of aridity—where shrimp,*

*tadpoles, and other ephemeral organisms develop in the aftermath of rain and snowmelt.*

"May your rivers flow without end...where something strange and more beautiful and more full of wonder than your deepest dreams waits for you...."

—EDWARD ABBEY

Colorado River slides through sunrise at Utah's Canyonlands National Park (above), where the Island in the Sky rises on the horizon. In another view of the same park—this one from the top looking down (opposite)—prince's plume graces the rim of Island in the Sky at Green River Overlook. The Colorado and Green Rivers converge in the heart of Canyonlands, drop into Cataract Canyon, and enter the waters of Lake Powell behind Glen Canyon Dam, the dam that broke Edward Abbey's heart.

FOLLOWING PAGES: Slickrock in a slot canyon tells of water's flash dance on sedimentary stone, creating a fantasy of form and color. It is uncertain how many slot canyons exist, or where. Among Abbey's legions of followers who explore them, a rule prevails: Don't tell. True hearts and strong legs will find slot canyons—by serendipity and magic.

# LISTEN TO THE LAND, ELOQUENTLY

# Biodiversity and the Geography of Hope

MARJORY
STONEMAN DOUGLAS

The governor of Florida was a busy man. Meetings, public appearances, and travel filled his week. An outer circle of aides and an inner circle of confidants assiduously protected his time and priorities. Getting a personal audience with him was not easy. Most callers would share a pleasantry or two, quickly state their cases, and depart with deferential handshakes while the governor maintained a subtle yet suitable posture of prestige.

Not this time. The woman who shuffled into his office was scarcely five feet tall and was 100 years old—a living legend. She wore a broad-brimmed hat, a cotton dress, and sturdy brown shoes. The governor greeted her warmly at the door and escorted her to a comfortable chair opposite his desk. Her name was Marjory Stoneman Douglas, and she got right to the point: the Everglades.

The future of the Everglades was the future of Florida, she said. If the Everglades died, so would Florida.

The governor agreed.

She didn't mean just Everglades National Park, mind you; she meant the entire Everglades ecosystem, an area several times larger than the park—a broad sheet of flowing water roughly 50 miles wide and 6 inches deep that moved slowly yet inexorably across the southern third of Florida, from Lake Okeechobee to Florida Bay.

"There are no other Everglades in the world," she wrote in her now classic book, *The Everglades: River of Grass*, published in 1947. "They are, they have always been, one of the unique regions of the earth, remote, never wholly known. Nothing anywhere else is like them: their vast glittering openness, wider than the enormous visible round of the horizon, the racing free saltness and sweetness of their massive winds, under the dazzling blue heights of space. They are unique also in the simplicity, the diversity, the related harmony of the forms of life they enclose. The miracle of the light pours over the green and brown expanse of saw grass and of water, shining and slow-moving below, the grass and water that

*Called the engineers of the Everglades, alligators dig holes that help marsh snails, frogs, and fish survive dry seasons, thus supporting ecological balance.*

*PRECEDING PAGES: Sentinel-like cypresses rise in Big Cypress National Preserve, which buffers beleaguered Everglades National Park to its south.*

is the meaning and the central fact of the Everglades of Florida."

A hundred years earlier, descriptions of the area were not so kind or enlightened. "Wholly valueless," said Florida's first state legislature. Time to ditch, dike, and drain "the swamp." Countless South Florida politicians won elections by campaigning to convert the pagan Everglades into pious farms, housing tracts, and shopping malls—the new Florida. The Army Corps of Engineers and other agencies straitjacketed meandering waterways into some 1,400 miles of levees and canals. Farmers converted grasslands into sugarcane and tomato fields. Miami swelled. By 1990, more than 5,000 people were moving into Florida each week, prompting one news columnist to suggest that the entire state, barely above water, might soon sink.

And the Everglades today? Gone are 90 percent of the wading birds—the egrets, herons, and ibises—that in the tens of thousands darkened the dawn by their flight. Gone is the natural hydrology that nourished and cleansed grassland, mangrove, and slough.

Endangered or threatened are 14 species of wildlife, including the snail kite, southern bald eagle, American crocodile, loggerhead turtle, red-cockaded woodpecker, wood stork, and Florida panther. And added to those dire statistics are the countless native plants imperiled by toxic chemicals and aggressive exotic species.

"The Everglades: Dying for Help," warned the cover story of the April 1994 NATIONAL GEOGRAPHIC. "Everglades National Park has been dying for decades, its waters dirtied and diverted by development upstream. Task forces, technical reports, and talk have thus far failed to fix the problem. Maybe this land—rattlesnakes and all—is not so lovable; while our heads say ecosystem and biodiversity, our hearts still say swamp."

Will this be Florida's eulogy?

Marjory Stoneman Douglas stabbed the air with her bony finger and talked about the last time she saw a Florida panther. How many were left now, she wondered, fewer than 30? Not good—she shook her head—not good at all. She reminisced about arriving in Miami in 1915 as a newly divorced 25-year-old who went to work as a reporter for her father's newspaper, the *Miami Herald*. Those were the days.

Miami was just a sleepy town back then with some 5,000 people, no more. She never remarried—once was enough—and in 1926 built an English-style stucco cottage in Coconut Grove where she still lived. Miami was too crowded now, she said: too many people wanting too much water. Priorities needed to change. She believed there was still time to save the Everglades. All the basic ingredients were there; they just needed repairing. It would take diligence, hard work, education, and commitment, but it wasn't too late. Hope springs eternal.

The governor agreed. Who could argue with a 100-year-old woman who found in Florida what Ponce de Leon had missed: the fountain of youth. Who could argue with an icon, the little old lady whom a former governor had called "the poet, the sledgehammer advocate, the constant conscience of the Everglades for half a century."

"It is an article of faith in Florida, in the emerging urban giant carved from wild dunes and inaccessible swamps," Douglas (with writer Randy Lee Loftis) added to *River of Grass* nearly 40 years after its initial publica-

tion, "that events can be propelled fast enough to keep ahead of consequences.  A century after man first started to dominate the Everglades,
that progress has stumbled. Consequences have started to catch up. It is,
perhaps, an opportunity.  The great wet wilderness of South Florida need
not be degraded to a permanent state of mediocrity. If the people will it,
if they enforce their will on the managers of Florida's future, the Everglades can be restored to nature's design."

It has been observed, and not without irony, that to honor wild
America and let the wilderness live will be our most civilized act; that before
we subjugated each other, we subjugated the land—and still do. Wendell
Berry, the poet, novelist, and essayist who restores eroded hillsides and fields
on his Kentucky farm, has written, "We are a remnant people in a remnant
country."  Our finest nobility and final declaration of emancipation, he
believes, will be to free the land from our own narrow economics, to
stitch the remnants back together again, if possible, as the people of Florida
must do to save the Everglades—and perhaps themselves. "And the
world cannot be discovered by a journey of miles, no matter how long,"
Berry wrote in "The Unforeseen Wilderness," "but only by a spiritual
journey, a journey of one inch, very arduous and humbling and joyful,
by which we arrive at the ground at our feet, and learn to be at home."

In his essay "The Gift of Wilderness," historian, teacher, and novelist
Wallace Stegner wrote that Berry "represents one sort of refusal to go on
with the unsettling of America.…He has made the turn that the New
England Transcendentalists made long before him.…He knows as well as
they did that respect for nature is indivisible.  An old lady talking to her
houseplants, a weekend gardener planting marigolds among his carrots
and spinach, and a backpacker exultantly surveying a wilderness to whose
highest point he has just won, are all on the same wavelength. In all of them,
the religion of nature and the science of ecology meet.  Though they may
be Christians, they have left behind the Judeo-Christian tradition which puts
man at the center of the universe and gives him dominion over the beasts
of the field and the fowls of the air.  America has taught them something
besides the economics of liquidation and raid."

There's an old adage that says if you change the world of a child, you
change the world. Many Miami inner-city schoolchildren visit the Everglades
for the first time as part of a National Park Service environmental education program.  It is a Florida they have never seen before, one they can
barely comprehend. They want to know who put all the dirt on the road.
They sniff the pines. They dip their hands into a slough and touch a turtle.
A ranger/naturalist tells them the story of Frog Travolta and Alligator
Newton-John, a clever conservation takeoff on a Hollywood movie.
The children howl.  They think they've been entertained.

But in truth they've been introduced to field biology, hydrology, and
ecology. Looking out across the great saw grass prairie, they might
experience what Wallace Stegner calls the "bigness" outside themselves,
"the birth of awe" from which they will never recover.  Then they leave—
some reluctantly, some not.

Odds are they'll go to the new Florida instead: Universal Studios and
Disney World, whose annual visitation figures vastly exceed those of the
Everglades. That an amusement park should eclipse a national park does
not surprise today's evolutionary psychologists who study emotional

"It's not
a question
of if we
can save the
Everglades.
We must.
There is
no choice
to consider."

—MARJORY STONEMAN
DOUGLAS
*LOS ANGELES TIMES*

quotients and mismatch theory, and see social issues as reflections of dissonance between our modern environments and our ancestral ones. We're a society on the run. We work long hours, eat fast foods, watch bombardment TV, and spin at velocities many nuclear families cannot tolerate. "Instant gratification takes too long," quipped a contemporary author. In a world of information superhighways and virtual reality, who has time for existentialism in a flat, wet, buggy place at the bottom of Florida?

The Everglades has no monolithic mountains or tidewater glaciers. It has no towering redwoods, technicolor canyons, or clockwork geysers. It has space. It challenges us to see beyond the obvious, to slow down and find solace in the silence. It inverts our perceptions: the sky above as big as the land—bigger—with clouds like clipper ships 40,000 feet high. It has what old-timers on the western plains would call "the trick of quiet." Go out there, they'd say. Stay a week, a month. Sleep under the stars. Cook over a fire. Watch the world around you; see how it wobbles, twitches, and spins. Be alone but not lonely. Smell the distance. Listen. When you come out, you'll think you know the Everglades better, and you will. But what you'll really know better is yourself.

Chief Seattle told President Franklin Pierce nearly a century and a half ago, "This we know: The earth does not belong to man; man belongs to the earth....Man did not weave the web of life; he is merely a strand in it. Whatever he does to the web, he does to himself." This great leader of many tribes did not need science to sweeten his cup of nature. Nor did any other Native American teacher. Each conveyed his knowledge in story rather than statistics, with his hands, face, and voice creating scenes on the edge of firelight no less spellbinding than those created by the finest actors on the best stages in America. Indian children learned about Trickster Raven and Wounded Bear and every other animal that encircled and enriched them. "So that they will respect the land," Chief Seattle said, "tell your children that the earth is rich with the lives of our kin. Teach your children what we have taught our children, that the earth is our mother. Whatever befalls the earth befalls the sons of the earth."

Our vision of a wild America has become rooted in a vision of ourselves. Our national parks, preserves, monuments, forests, and wildlife refuges speak of gratitude and hope, renewal and redemption. They color our maps and minds and show we can make room for others. Most significant of all, they prove a rule in our democracy: That each new American generation will strive to extend to others the rights and freedoms held stubbornly by previous generations.

Heresy will become orthodoxy, but never without a struggle. Perhaps then, too, wilderness will become something as humane as it is natural, as much within us as it is around us.

Then our greatest learning will begin.

Numerous naturalists and scientists have said with glee that nature holds the answers to questions we've not yet learned to ask. This we already know: Ecosystems are more complex than we think—and are in fact more complex than we *can* think. Size is important. "If we are not able to safeguard wildlands in sufficiently big tracts," writes author and wildlife biologist Douglas H. Chadwick, "then the processes and patterns that shaped existing biological communities can no longer operate as they have for millions of years. And that would mark the end of natural history. From there

"We are still in transition from the notion of man as master of the earth to the notion of man as a part of it."

—WALLACE STEGNER
*WHERE THE BLUEBIRD SINGS TO THE LEMONADE SPRINGS*

on, we would be pinwheeling into an unfathomable era with no reference point other than the shifting impulses and convictions of humankind."

Island biogeography theory tells us that a natural area ten times larger than another area—everything else being equal—will contain roughly twice as many species. When postulated in the 1960s by ecologists R. H. MacArthur and E. O. Wilson, this theory was a fascinating academic exercise. In the last 30 years, however, especially the last 10, conservation biologists have found it applicable not just to ocean islands, but to any wild areas surrounded by development. They too are islands—ecological islands in seas of clearcuts, pipelines, fences, and concrete.

Development doesn't need to penetrate a wild area to damage its biological diversity; it can accomplish that simply by sprawling around it, insularizing it, intensifying its "island condition" by impeding if not occluding the natural free flow of wildlife in and out. The damage will not be severe at first, the theory tells us, and the area will be no smaller on a map. But over time—decades, maybe centuries—it will become a largely sterile vestige of its former genetic richness. Natural no more.

"Biological diversity must be treated more seriously as a global resource, to be indexed, used, and above all, preserved," writes E. O. Wilson, whose name has become synonymous with biodiversity. He warns us that now—just as science is unveiling the full diversity of plant and animal species around the world and its importance to our future global health—mankind is destroying that diversity with exploding human populations and habitat destruction, especially in the tropics.

"In the end," he writes, "I suspect it will all come down to a decision of ethics—how we value the natural worlds in which we evolved and now, increasingly, how we regard our status as individuals. We are fundamentally mammals and free spirits who reached this high a level of rationality by the perpetual creation of new options. Natural philosophy and science have brought into clear relief what might be the essential paradox of human existence. The drive toward perpetual expansion—or personal freedom—is basic to the human spirit. But to sustain it, we need the most delicate, knowing stewardship of the living world that can be devised."

A good beginning, say deep ecologists, is to live lightly and with respect for all living things, to leave our children a gift as rewarding as the one we received. "We need to learn to listen to the land," writes Wallace Stegner, "hear what it says, understand what it can and can't do over the long haul."

David Brower, the environmental archdruid who founded Friends of the Earth, the League of Conservation Voters, and the Earth Island Institute, agrees with Stegner and adds that we should "listen eloquently....A tough reappraisal of progress is overdue. Unquestioned growth is not part of it....We ought not to be blindly against progress, but against blind progress, and to try to distinguish one from the other, which few people do."

Students of environmentalism say many American jewels—Denali, Glen Canyon, Big Bend, the Maine woods, Yellowstone, the Florida Keys—have already been won or lost, though winning is an illusion, since the threats never go away. Every defeat is final, they say; every victory, provisional.

Yet small pieces of natural habitat, like small children, can make a big difference, for as they grow we become aware of their importance. They

*FOLLOWING PAGES: Speared sunfish in its bill, an anhinga has risen to the surface after stalking its prey underwater. In the Everglades the dramas of predator and prey unfold daily before visitors' eyes. One of the more popular spots in the park is the Anhinga Trail where mornings dawn to a cacophony of birds calling, alligators bellowing, and turtles splashing in a slough.*

GEORGE J. SANKER/DRK PHOTO

"While, we were working so ruthlessly on the
It built something into our national
finally teaches us...responsibility, for wilderness, once

sustain the remnants of Wendell Berry's America, remnants that can someday develop and coalesce into true wilderness. Many small but critical habitats provide natural corridors that allow wildlife to migrate between larger areas. The Backyard Habitat Campaign of the National Wildlife Federation is just one of dozens of programs that give millions of Americans a chance to reconstruct a more natural environment around their homes: to replant native brush, for example, and the next spring find a family of goldfinches nesting in it.

By accident, reprieve, enlightenment, and luck, the fallen forests of the eastern United States have risen again. Wild woods now cover 60 percent of southern New England, 80 percent of Vermont, and 90 percent of New Hampshire.

Bill McKibben wrote in the *Atlantic Monthly*, "Here, where 'suburb' and 'megalopolis' were added to the world's vocabulary, an explosion of green is under way, one that could offer hope to much of the rest of the planet."

The descendants of wildlife that long ago perished before rifle, ax, and plow now stand ready to return. They smell a new America—one for the sharing. In 1987, 400 years after Virginia Dare became the first child born to English parents in the New World—on Roanoke Island, in what is now North Carolina—a team of U.S. Fish and Wildlife Service biologists released a pair of radio-collared red wolves into that island's Alligator River National Wildlife Refuge. "The animals disappeared into the woods perhaps half an hour's drive from the spot where Dare was born," wrote McKibben. "The species was the first ever to go extinct in the North American wild and then be reintroduced into the natural world from a remnant population in zoos. They were, as surely as Dare, pioneers."

By 1995, 61 wild-born red wolf pups belonged to the Roanoke Island pack. Their howls filled the night. All across America, from rural uplands to deep woods to ragged western mountains, the stories are the same: tracks in the mud and tales in the taverns speak of mountain lions, grizzly bears, and coyotes. They're back—and with them an energy, vitality, and national youth we thought we'd lost.

Yet while the fertile East forgives us, the arid West does not.

"You have to get over the color green…," Wallace Stegner observed in his final book of nonfiction, *Where the Bluebird Sings to the Lemonade Springs*. "You have to quit associating beauty with gardens and lawns; you have to get used to an inhuman scale.…The deserts were doing all right until we came along and set out to reform them. Making them blossom is something we inherited from Isaiah." This pump-the-well-dry approach is what Stegner says makes the Westerner "less a person than a continuing adaptation," and the West "less a place than a process."

wilderness, it was working on us....
memory....Curiously, it may be the love of wilderness that
our parent..., has become our dependent.

—WALLACE STEGNER
*THE GIFT OF WILDERNESS*

Himself a Westerner, he grew up on the move as his father chased rainbows and mirages and dragged his family along with him. *The Big Rock Candy Mountain,* Stegner's first novel, recounts his father's world-owes-me-a-bonanza attitude, and how "he died broke and friendless in a fleabag hotel, having in his lifetime done more human and environmental damage than he could have repaired in a second lifetime.... There are plenty of people in the West—millions, probably—who still think like my father, and who approach western land, water, grass, timber, mineral resources, and scenery as grave robbers might approach the tomb of a pharaoh."

The truth can hurt, as it must have hurt Stegner when adulthood provided him a clear lens to see his father's folly. Yet perhaps because he swallowed his truth whole, it gave him voice; he leavened wisdom, criticized corporate despotism, and gave hope to millions. He won a Pulitzer Prize and a National Book Award and founded a writing program at Stanford University that helped launch the writers of the purple sage—a genre dedicated more to place than process. "I feel the surge of the inextinguishable western hope," he wrote shortly before his death in 1993 at age 84. "It is a civilization they are building, a history they are compiling, a way of looking at the world and humanity's place in it. I think they will do it."

Hope springs eternal.

If historian/philosopher Henry Adams was right in saying that chaos is the law of nature and that order is the dream of man, then as Stegner-admirer and author Barry Lopez has written: "One of the great dreams of man must be to find some place between the extremes of nature and civilization where it is possible to live without regret."

Many preservationists did. Henry David Thoreau found inspiration at Walden Pond, yet frequently walked into Concord to visit family and friends. Ralph Waldo Emerson urged John Muir to return East with him from Yosemite, saying wilderness was a sublime mistress but an intolerant wife. Bob Marshall found reflective hours back in his cabin a perfect complement to the Arctic adventures that chilled and thrilled him. To Rachel Carson both seashores and libraries were sanctuaries.

For all her years Marjory Stoneman Douglas spent little time in the Everglades. She didn't need to, she said; she found peace just knowing it was there—a once and future Florida blessed with water and roofed with birds. It was her touchstone, her cradle of conservation, what Wallace Stegner would call her "geography of hope." The Everglades was orphaned and she adopted it, proving that compassion is not weakness and that profit is not virtue. Ask any recent Florida governor.

Marjory Stoneman Douglas and others like her, from Thoreau to Stegner, gave us their deepest fears but also their brightest hopes—their visions of a wild America.

*S*taring back from the edge of oblivion, the Florida panther (opposite) now numbers probably fewer than 30 animals in the wild. Perhaps, as some biologists say, too few exist in this population to maintain its genetic viability. A single disease could wipe them out. Intensified conservation efforts aim to rebuff increasing human pressures until a new day can dawn for the Everglades (below), and its wild systems can be restored to a stronger semblance of their original heartbeats.

PRECEDING PAGES: Big Cypress National Preserve adjoins the Everglades, which remains the largest national park in the eastern United States. "Everglades National Park, and places like it," writes senior park biologist William B. Robertson, Jr., "exist because we dimly realize that we are yet too close to real frontiers and all of our beginnings to thrive indefinitely in a world of asphalt and concrete."

*L*ittle more than four inches long, the black-tailed gnatcatcher makes its
home in both the Mojave and Sonoran deserts of southern California and Arizona,
and also dwells deep into Mexico, down the full length of Baja California.
Yet the coastal California variety of this bird—regarded by many authorities as
a separate species—is endangered and loses more habitat

every year to exploding human populations and rampant development.
Conservationists ask whether a world consumed with dollars and cents, black and
white, Democrat and Republican, can protect the future of
a little bird in a little corner of America, where it has lived for countless ages.
If not, then what of big birds? And mammals? And ourselves?

*PRECEDING PAGES: Snow geese enliven a winter day at Bosque del Apache National Wildlife Refuge in central New Mexico. Come spring, they will fly north to breed in Arctic Alaska and Canada. Because birds fly, migrate, and sing, come in many sizes, shapes, and colors, and seem to possess magic and mystery, they have won the hearts of tens of millions of bird lovers. And because they travel—some of them great distances—birds serve as indicators of environmental health and as ambassadors between the artificial worlds we've made and the natural world we come from.*

*An American symbol and success story, the bald eagle (above) has rebounded from the endangered species list throughout the lower 48 states, its breeding pairs up from about 400 in the early 1960s to 4,000 in the mid-1990s. Other species have not fared so well: the passenger pigeon, the heath hen, the emerald trout. Roughly 500 species and subspecies of North American plants and animals have disappeared since Columbus splashed ashore—an average of one a year. Thousands of others teeter on the edge. We are just beginning to learn that places once considered useless, such as the wetlands of New Jersey's Great Swamp National Wildlife Refuge (left), are in fact critical habitats that sustain valuable pieces of a fractured but still living wild America.*

"In meeting the
revised needs of man,
we are saving
some unrevised
works of God."

—DAVID BROWER, *FOR EARTH'S SAKE*

PAUL CHESLEY

*Paraded by environmentalists*
*and parodied by loggers, the northern*
*spotted owl (above) has become*
*a lightning rod of contentious debate,*
*symbolizing the power and weight of*
*the 1973 Endangered Species Act. The*
*owl requires old-growth forests (right) to*
*survive. While some say it's a question*
*of owls against jobs, others say it's deeper.*
*"When the last individual of a race*
*of living things breathes no more," wrote*
*naturalist William Beebe, "another*
*heaven and another earth must pass*
*before such a one can be again."*

*FOLLOWING PAGES: Cathedral of trees*
*and moss, the Hoh Rain Forest of*
*Washington State's Olympic National*
*Park preserves a shrinking habitat.*

TERRY DONNELLY (RIGHT), CHARLES GURCHE (FOLLOWING PAGES)

*In southeast Alaska's Tongass National Forest, waterfalls pour into Punchbowl Lake, Misty Fiords National Monument (left). Bunchberries brighten the forest floor on Mitkof Island (below).*

*FOLLOWING PAGES: Caribou from the Porcupine Caribou Herd migrate through the Hulahula River Valley in Alaska's Arctic National Wildlife Refuge. For generations they have walked these northern contours, the females giving birth every summer on the refuge's coastal plain, precisely where industry now wants to drill for oil. This strongly desired landscape has become an Arctic grail, the focus of one of the last great American wilderness debates of the 20th century. In time Congress will either bow to industrialists' dreams of billions of barrels of oil and allow drilling, or to conservationists' pleas to protect forever what U.S. Secretary of the Interior Bruce Babbitt called, "this ancient pageant of wildlife moving through the seasons of an enchanted landscape."*

# Index

## Author's Note

A former park ranger in Alaska's Glacier Bay, Denali, and Katmai National Parks, Kim Heacox lives in southeast Alaska with his wife, Melanie, their sea kayaks, a vegetable garden, and the rain. A fascination with natural history has taken him on assignment to Africa, the Galápagos, the Arctic, and the Antarctic. He has twice won the Lowell Thomas Award for excellence in travel journalism, and his book *IN DENALI* won the Benjamin Franklin Award. Kim Heacox recently completed his first novel, *AN HONEST PLACE,* about political intrigue and Alaska's Arctic National Wildlife Refuge.

## Acknowledgments

The Book Division and the author wish to thank the many individuals, groups, and organizations mentioned or quoted in this publication for their help and guidance. We are especially grateful to the following individuals and organizations:

The Aldo Leopold Foundation, Diane Allen, Charles Bradley, Nina Leopold Bradley, Nancy Brown, Don Congdon Associates, Inc., Linda Eade, the Edward Abbey Estate, Brent Haglund, Taher Husain, Kevin McAleese, Jonathan Marshall, Lisa Peacock, John Quinley, the Rachel Carson Council, the Sand County Foundation, Allen Smith, the Wilderness Society, and Larry Vancour.

Excerpts from *Desert Solitaire* reprinted by permission of Don Congdon Associates, Inc. Copyright © 1968 by Edward Abbey, renewed 1996 by Clarke Abbey.

PHOTOGRAPH BY MELANIE HEACOX

## Additional Reading

**Edward Abbey,** *Abbey's Road; Beyond the Wall; The Brave Cowboy; Desert Solitaire; The Fool's Progress; Hayduke Lives!; The Monkey Wrench Gang; One Life at a Time, Please*
**Rachel Carson,** *The Edge of the Sea, The Sea Around Us, The Sense of Wonder, Silent Spring*
**Marjory Stoneman Douglas,** *The Everglades: River of Grass, Voice of the River*
**Aldo Leopold,** *A Sand County Almanac, Round River*
**Robert Marshall,** *Alaska Wilderness, Arctic Village*
**John Muir,** *My First Summer in the Sierra, Our National Parks, The Story of My Boyhood and Youth, Travels in Alaska*
**Wallace Stegner,** *All the Little Live Things, Angle of Repose, Beyond the Hundredth Meridian, The Big Rock Candy Mountain, The Spectator Bird, Where the Bluebird Sings to the Lemonade Springs*
**Henry David Thoreau,** *Walden*

Visit the Society's Web site at http://www.nationalgeographic.com or at GO NATIONAL GEOGRAPHIC on CompuServe.

**Library of Congress ℂℙ Data**

Heacox, Kim.
    Visions of a wild America : pioneers of preservation / by Kim Heacox.
        p.   cm.
    "Prepared by the Book Division."
    Includes bibliographical references (p.      ) and index.
    ISBN 0-7922-2944-4 (reg. edition).  — ISBN 0-7922-2974-6 (deluxe)
    1. Naturalists—United States—Biography.
2. Conservationists—United States—Biography.
3. Nature conservation—United States—History.
4. Natural history—United States. 5. Natural history—United States—Pictorial works. I. National Geographic Society (U.S.). Book Division. II. Title.
    QH26.H38  1996
    333.7'2'0973—dc20                    96-18715

                                        ℂℙ

Composition for this book done by the National Geographic Society Book Division. Printed and bound by R. R. Donnelley & Sons, Willard, Ohio. Color separations by Digital Color Image, Pennsauken, N.J. Dust jacket printed by Miken Systems, Inc., Cheektowaga, N.Y.